JANE AUSTEN

W9-ATH-975

COMPREHENSIVE RESEARCH
AND STUDY GUIDE

BLOOM'S

MAJOR

NOVELISTS

EDITED AND WITH AN
INTRODUCTION BY HAROLD BLOOM

BLOOM'S MAJOR DRAMATISTS

Anton Chekhov

Henrik Ibsen

Arthur Miller

Eugene O'Neill

Shakespeare's Comedies

Shakespeare's Histories

Shakespeare's Romances

Shakespeare's Tragedies

George Bernard Shaw

Tennessee Williams

BLOOM'S MAJOR NOVELISTS

Jane Austen

The Brontës

Willa Cather

Charles Dickens

William Faulkner

F. Scott Fitzgerald

Nathaniel Hawthorne

Ernest Hemingway

Toni Morrison

John Steinbeck

Mark Twain

Alice Walker

BLOOM'S MAJOR SHORT STORY WRITERS

William Faulkner

F. Scott Fitzgerald

Ernest Hemingway

O. Henry

James Joyce

Herman Melville

Flannery O'Connor

Edgar Allan Poe

J. D. Salinger

John Steinbeck

Mark Twain

Eudora Welty

BLOOM'S MAJOR WORLD POETS

Geoffrey Chaucer

Emily Dickinson

John Donne

T. S. Eliot

Robert Frost

Langston Hughes

John Milton

Edgar Allan Poe

Shakespeare's Poems & Sonnets

Alfred, Lord Tennyson

Walt Whitman

William Wordsworth

BLOOM'S NOTES

The Adventures of Huckleberry Finn

Aeneid

The Age of Innocence

Animal Farm

The Autobiography of Malcolm X

The Awakening

Beloved

Beowulf

Billy Budd, Benito Cereno, & Bartleby the Scrivener

Brave New World

The Catcher in the Rye

Crime and Punishment

The Crucible

Death of a Salesman

A Farewell to Arms

Frankenstein

The Grapes of Wrath

Great Expectations

The Great Gatsby

Gulliver's Travels

Hamlet

Heart of Darkness & The Secret Sharer

Henry IV, Part One

I Know Why the Caged Bird Sings

Iliad

Inferno

Invisible Man

Jane Eyre

Julius Caesar

King Lear

Lord of the Flies

Macbeth

A Midsummer Night's Dream

Moby-Dick

Native Son

Nineteen Eighty-Four

Odyssey

Oedipus Plays

Of Mice and Men

The Old Man and the Sea

Othello

Paradise Lost

The Portrait of a Lady

A Portrait of the Artist as a Young Man

Pride and Prejudice

The Red Badge of Courage

Romeo and Juliet

The Scarlet Letter

Silas Marner

The Sound and the Fury

The Sun Also Rises

A Tale of Two Cities

Tess of the D'Urbervilles

Their Eyes Were Watching God

To Kill a Mockingbird

Uncle Tom's Cabin

Wuthering Heights

JANE AUSTEN

COMPREHENSIVE RESEARCH
AND STUDY GUIDE

BLOOM'S
MAJOR
NOVELISTS

EDITED AND WITH AN INTRODUCTION
BY HAROLD BLOOM

First Printing
1 3 5 7 9 8 6 4 2

Library of Congress Cataloging-in-Publication Data

Jane Austen / edited and with an introduction by Harold Bloom.
p.   cm.—(Bloom's major novelists)
Includes bibliographical references and index.
ISBN 0-7910-5260-5 (hc)
1. Austen, Jane, 1775–1817—Examinations—Study guides.
I. Bloom, Harold.   II. Series.
PR4037.J28   1999
823'.7—dc21
99-29497
CIP

Chelsea House Publishers
1974 Sproul Road, Suite 400
Broomall, PA 19008-0914

The Chelsea House World Wide Website address is
http://www.chelseahouse.com

Contributing Editor: Barbara Fischer

Contents

User's Guide

This volume is designed to present biographical, critical, and bibliographical information on the playwright's best-known or most important works. Following Harold Bloom's editor's note and introduction are a detailed biography of the author, discussing major life events and important literary accomplishments. A plot summary of each play follows, tracing significant themes, patterns, and motifs in the work.

A selection of critical extracts, derived from previously published material from leading critics, analyzes aspects of each play. The extracts consist of statements from the author, if available, early reviews of the work, and later evaluations up to the present. A bibliography of the author's writings (including a complete list of all works written, cowritten, edited, and translated), a list of additional books and articles on the author and his or her work, and an index of themes and ideas in the author's writings conclude the volume.

~

Harold Bloom is Sterling Professor of the Humanities at Yale University and Henry W. and Albert A. Berg Professor of English at the New York University Graduate School. He is the author of over 20 books and the editor of more than 30 anthologies of literary criticism.

Professor Bloom's works include *Shelley's Mythmaking* (1959), *The Visionary Company* (1961), *Blake's Apocalypse* (1963), *Yeats* (1970), *A Map of Misreading* (1975), *Kabbalah and Criticism* (1975), and *Agon: Toward a Theory of Revisionism* (1982). *The Anxiety of Influence* (1973) sets forth Professor Bloom's provocative theory of the literary relationships between the great writers and their predecessors. His most recent books include *The American Religion* (1992), *The Western Canon* (1994), *Omens of Millennium: The Gnosis of Angels, Dreams, and Resurrection* (1996), and *Shakespeare: The Invention of the Human* (1998), a finalist for the 1998 National Book Award.

Professor Bloom earned his Ph.D. from Yale University in 1955 and has served on the Yale faculty since then. He is a 1985 MacArthur Foundation Award recipient, served as the Charles Eliot Norton Professor of Poetry at Harvard University in 1987–88, and has received honorary degrees from the universities of Rome and Bologna. In 1999, Professor Bloom received the prestigious American Academy of Arts and Letters Gold Medal for Criticism.

Currently, Harold Bloom is the editor of numerous Chelsea House volumes of literary criticism, including the series BLOOM'S NOTES, BLOOM'S MAJOR SHORT STORY WRITERS, BLOOM'S MAJOR POETS, MAJOR LITERARY CHARACTERS, MODERN CRITICAL VIEWS, MODERN CRITICAL INTERPRETATIONS, and WOMEN WRITERS OF ENGLISH AND THEIR WORKS.

Editor's Note

The twenty-six Critical Views excerpted in this little volume are too varied for easy summary. I myself am particularly moved and instructed by Henry James and A. Walton Litz on *Sense and Sensibility*, and by Austen herself and Ian Watt on *Pride and Prejudice.*

Mansfield Park seems to me remarkably illuminated by Mary Poovey and Edward Said, while *Emma* is fascinatingly perspectivized by Marvin Mudrick, Wayne Booth, and Susan Morgan.

Tony Tanner shrewdly investigates problems of identity in *Persuasion,* a book difficult to characterize but helpfully commented upon here by all the critics cited.

Introduction

HAROLD BLOOM

In the Dark Ages ahead of us, when the visual media will reduce everything to virtual reality, Jane Austen will survive, together with Shakespeare and Dickens. These seem the three great writers in the language who require least mediation; the reader happily can be alone with them, whatever the circumstances that work against deep contemplation or that deny us an informed solitude. It is a cultural tragedy that difficult writers who demand learned mediation, from Dante through John Milton to James Joyce, may vanish except for elite handfuls of readers. Austen, like Shakespeare and Dickens, will carry the aesthetic and cognitive values of the highest literary art even into a cosmos dominated by the tyranny of the bodily eye.

Shakespeare, though the richest of all imaginations, conveyed much of his art through ellipsis, exclusion, and a complex fore-grounding. Jane Austen, the most Shakespearean of all novelists, follows Shakespeare in many ways, though clearly the surface of her art is far more exclusionary than his. Her principal resource is irony, exquisitely modulated, while Shakespeare's resources are so varied that irony is only one element among many. Yet Austen's irony is clearly learned from Shakespeare; it is Rosalind's wit, in *As You Like It*, that is the ultimate of Jane Austen's inventiveness in the ironic mode.

Difficult as it is to name Austen's masterpiece among her four greatest novels—*Pride and Prejudice, Mansfield Park, Emma,* and *Persuasion* (my personal favorite)—the public always has particularly esteemed *Pride and Prejudice*. The extended mutual path to an accurate recognition of one another journeyed by Elizabeth and Darcy is the formal center of the book, and maintains a continuous Shakespearean exuberance. Surprise is as much Austen's resource as it is the particular strength of Shakespearean comedy. So is the crucial importance of the unsaid, also learned by Austen from Shakespeare.

What is unique to Austen, and not at all Shakespearean, is her reliance upon her personal, largely secularized sense of the Protestant will, which is a will to self-esteem, rather than Falstaff's will to live or Macbeth's will to power. Elizabeth and Darcy share at last in a proper pride, the pride of returned self-estimates. Each has maintained the right of self-judgment in regard to the other, and to all others.

Ultimately, Austen's heroines—Elizabeth, Emma, Fanny Price in *Mansfield Park*, Anne Elliot in *Persuasion*—are grand normative sensibilities, descendants of *As You Like It*'s wonderful Rosalind. Psychic health and good will are not qualities at all easy to represent in literature, let alone represent with depth, intensity, and aesthetic rightness. Jane Austen deeply shares in Shakespeare's rare power at achieving such representation, and she remains the most Shakespearean novelist in the language. ❀

Biography of
Jane Austen

Jane Austen, the seventh of eight children, was born on December 16, 1775, in the village of Steventon in Hampshire, England. Her father, Reverend George Austen, was the parish clergyman, and her mother, Cassandra Leigh Austen, was the daughter of a clergyman from a well-connected family. Austen and her sister Cassandra received some early education from the widow of a principal of Brasenose College in Oxford and in Southampton, and later enrolled briefly in the Abbey School in Reading. After the age of nine, Austen was educated at home in the rectory, learning French, Italian, music, and needlework, and reading extensively. Her favorite books included the novels of Samuel Richardson, Henry Fielding, and Fanny Burney, the poetry of William Cowper, and the essays of Samuel Johnson.

Austen stated that for a novelist "three or four families in a country village is the very thing to work on," and she grew up among the clergy and minor landed gentry in communities resembling those portrayed in her novels. She began writing in her early adolescence to entertain her family, composing humorous sketches and parodies of sentimental novels. The family would stage plays and farces in the barn, including some of her own dramatic pieces. Between ages 14 and 16, she wrote a novel, the satirical *Love and Friendship,* which can be found in her three-volume *Juvenilia.* Around age 20, Austen wrote two epistolary novels, *Lady Susan* and *Elinor and Marianne,* the latter of which became *Sense and Sensibility.* A year later, she wrote *First Impressions,* an early version of *Pride and Prejudice,* which her father attempted, unsuccessfully, to have published. She also wrote *Susan,* an early version of *Northanger Abbey,* parodying the conventions of Gothic novels.

In 1801, Austen and her family moved to Bath in hopes of restoring her father's health. The move initiated a difficult period for her, uprooting her from her familiar and beloved home. At this time, she likely had several suitors, and by some accounts met and fell in love with a man who returned her feelings, but who died soon thereafter of a sudden illness. In 1802, Austen accepted a proposal of marriage from Harris Bigg-Wither, but changed her mind after a sleepless night. She remained unmarried.

Facing the disappointments and personal losses of this period, including the sudden death of a close friend, Austen wrote much less. In 1803, she sold *Susan* to a London publisher for £10, but it was never printed. She wrote ten chapters of a novel, *The Watsons,* but abandoned the work when her father died in 1805. His death brought financial instability as well as tremendous grief to Austen, her mother, and her sister. After living in various temporary lodgings in Bath for a year, struggling to accumulate a basic income from family sources, they moved to be near Austen's brother Frank in Southampton, a city in which Austen was lonely and unhappy.

In 1809, the three women moved to Chawton Cottage, part of Austen's brother Edward's estate in Hampshire. "Barton Cottage" in *Sense and Sensibility* is said to resemble it. Here, Austen renewed work on her novels and began writing prolifically. She revised *Sense and Sensibility,* publishing it anonymously at her own expense in 1811, and it received favorable reviews. She then rewrote *First Impressions,* and it appeared as *Pride and Prejudice* in January 1813. *Mansfield Park* was published the following May. By the end of 1815, Austen had completed *Emma* and begun *Persuasion.* The novels achieved modest success, going into second and third printings. George, Prince of Wales, who ruled for King George III as the Prince Regent from 1811 to 1820, became an admirer of Austen's novels, and she dedicated *Emma* to him when it was published anonymously in December 1815, by Lord Byron's publisher, John Murray.

In 1816, Austen bought the rights to *Susan* back from Crosby of London and rewrote it as *Northanger Abbey.* In this year, with the onset of her fatal illness, she also wrote the burlesque *Plan of a Novel* and began *Sanditon,* a satire on spa towns and invalidism. She suffered from Addison's disease, a progressive atrophy of the adrenal gland that causes a lack of vital hormones, and died in Winchester on July 18, 1817, at age 41. She was buried in Winchester Cathedral. In 1818, *Persuasion* and *Northanger Abbey* were published, also anonymously, but her authorship was made public in a biographical note by her brother Henry.

Living a quiet, retired life, Austen recorded her milieu with shrewd insight and wit. As familiar as the characters in her comedies of manners come to seem to us, they nonetheless represent a particular middle-class social structure and a historical period very different from our own. From smaller matters, such as ways of mailing letters, modes of travel, and forms of address (for example, Elinor Dashwood, an oldest daughter, is addressed as "Miss Dashwood," the younger Marianne Dashwood as "Miss Marianne"), to larger concerns of rank, inheritance, educational philosophies, and roles for women, Austen's novels open myriad opportunities for examining historical and social issues.

Her novels also present an artistic achievement and innovation of the first order. More than any writer before her, Austen utilized and perfected what has been termed "free indirect discourse," a narrative technique that allows a third-person omniscient narrator to speak the feelings and perceptions of the characters, allowing us "into their heads," while at the same time maintaining distance to comment upon, with irony, their behaviors. Early criticism labeled Austen a "miniaturist" (as she labeled herself) or a "merely domestic" novelist, but she was soon thereafter assessed to be the most important novelist of the Regency period.

Austen appears in several contradictory guises in twentieth-century criticism. Is she conservative or shaking the foundations of conservatism? Affirmative of her social order or subversive? A reactionary or a reformist? As Claudia Johnson observes in *Jane Austen: Women, Politics, and the Novel*, she is portrayed by different critics "as a cameoist oblivious to her times, or a stern propagandist on behalf of a beleaguered ruling class; as a self-effacing good aunt, or a nasty old maid; as a subtly discriminating stylist, or a homely song bird, unconscious of her art." Regardless of the critical stance that is taken, however, Austen's skill at sympathetic characterization, her realistic treatment of everyday life, and her deft command of the comic, make her indisputably one of the most admired and beloved of all novelists. ❀

Plot Summary of
Sense and Sensibility

When Austen contrasts Elinor's "sense," her practical, clear-sighted judgment and command of her feelings, with Marianne's "sensibility," her emotional intensity and belief that her feelings should guide her actions, she follows a popular convention for didactic novels of the late eighteenth century. The personalities of the two sisters are not strictly antithetical, however, as Austen modifies conventional character types with subtle irony. As both Elinor and Marianne suffer disappointment in love and sustain the warmth of their close relationship, they undergo transformations that would not be possible without a mix of "sense" and "sensibility." Both must learn to mediate between their individual desires, their need to love and be loved, and the claims of family and society.

After their father's death, the Dashwood sisters and their mother are left in financial difficulty. Most of the Norland estate has been left to their half-brother, Mr. John Dashwood, and he is convinced by his selfish wife, Fanny, not to concern himself with financial assistance for his sisters, despite his father's deathbed wish. At this time, Elinor meets Edward Ferrars, Fanny's brother, and they develop a close friendship, much to Fanny's chagrin. Elinor has strong feelings for him, but admits only that she "likes" him, incurring the friendly ridicule of her mother and sister, who insist on a more romantic notion of love. Edward, though virtuous, is not striking or passionate.

Uncomfortable staying with John and Fanny at Norland, Mrs. Dashwood and her three daughters (the youngest, Margaret, is 13) move to Barton Cottage in Devonshire, part of the property of Sir John Middleton, a distant relative. Austen wittily evokes the provincial society they encounter, especially in the comic portrait of Sir Middleton's mother-in-law, Mrs. Jennings. The Dashwoods are a welcome addition to this small social circle, and Mrs. Jennings embarrasses them with matchmaking attempts. Marianne is admired by Colonel Brandon, a dignified, wealthy landowner, but she dismisses him as "infirm" and unsuitable for matrimony, since he is over 35.

Marianne soon finds a love interest of more suitably romantic proportions. Caught in a rainstorm while out walking, she slips and twists her ankle. She is carried home by the dashing John Willoughby, whose "person and air were equal to what her fancy had ever drawn for the hero of a favourite story," and promptly falls in love with him. Reading poetry, playing music, and going out riding together, they relish their desire to flaunt conventional decorum and live passionately. The attachment appears serious to all who know them, and they are presumed to be engaged. One country excursion is cut short, however, when Colonel Brandon leaves abruptly on serious business, an uneasy moment that foreshadows trouble. Not long afterward, Willoughby himself departs hastily for London, a circumstance that causes Elinor to doubt his constancy and integrity, as no engagement between him and Marianne has been openly declared. Elinor assumes that they must have reached an understanding for Marianne to behave so freely with him.

Several visitors bring new possibilities as well as fresh disappointments to the Dashwood sisters. Edward visits Barton Cottage, but his aloof behavior is perplexing and Elinor cannot be sure of his feelings. The giddy Mrs. Palmer, Mrs. Jennings's daughter, arrives with her "droll" and sour husband, providing ample comic material and further embarrassment for the well-educated and polite Dashwoods. The ill-bred Miss Steeles, who ingratiate themselves with the Middletons, also enliven the neighborhood. Lucy Steele, "illiterate, artful, and selfish," suspects Elinor's affection for Edward and confides that she has been secretly engaged to him for four years, since he was a student living with Lucy's uncle. Elinor is heartbroken, but conceals her feelings from everyone, keeping her promise of secrecy to Lucy.

As **Volume II** opens, the unhappy but sensible Elinor believes that she was not deceived by Edward and refuses to blame him. We later learn that Edward clearly regrets his attachment to Lucy, formed when he was young and inexperienced, but Elinor quietly resigns herself to the knowledge that his high principles will not allow him to break his engagement. Marianne, by contrast, is openly anxious and distraught in Willoughby's absence, and readily accepts Mrs. Jennings's invitation for her and Elinor to spend the fall season in London. When they arrive, Marianne writes several desperate letters, but Willoughby does not visit. They meet unexpectedly at a ball, where Willoughby coldly rebuffs Marianne's greeting, and we soon discover that he is engaged to the fabulously wealthy Miss Grey.

He sends Marianne an "impudently cruel" letter claiming that any suggestion of commitment he displayed in Devonshire was "perfectly unintentional." Marianne confesses to Elinor that she was never actually engaged to him, that "it was every day implied, but never professedly declared." Marianne is crushed by his betrayal, and remains despondent for many weeks.

Believing that he can ease Marianne's pain in the long run, Colonel Brandon relates his own story to Elinor. He tells of his early love for a woman named Eliza, a rich orphan cousin who grew up with him. He and Eliza longed to marry, but she was forced to marry his older brother to save the family from financial decline. The "misery of her situation" led her to leave her husband, and she fell into "a life of sin." Colonel Brandon found her again only as she was dying, and vowed to care for her illegitimate child. Though educated under Brandon's protection, this child, now grown, has recently fallen into disgrace as well—with John Willoughby. She bears his child, but Willoughby refuses to take responsibility, a circumstance that provoked Colonel Brandon's sudden departure from Devonshire several months before.

Throughout her time in London, Elinor is forced to tolerate the impertinent Lucy Steele, who continues to talk to her about Edward. Envious of Elinor's grace, Lucy does whatever she can to upset her. Edward's mother, meanwhile, is arranging for him to marry a rich woman. In **Volume III,** Lucy and Edward's secret engagement becomes public, and his family is outraged. When Edward honorably refuses to break the engagement, he is disowned. All the family property is settled on his irresponsible brother Robert. Marianne is astonished to learn that Elinor has known of Edward's engagement for so long. She cannot believe that Elinor has withstood teasing about him and never revealed her own sadness. Comparing Elinor's fortitude with her own lavish displays of grief, she is ashamed.

Colonel Brandon, understanding familial unfairness in matters of marriage and money too well, gives Edward a living as the curate of his parish, a basic income that enables him to marry Lucy. Elinor assumes that their marriage will soon take place, and once again keeps her disappointment in check. Elinor and Marianne return home by way of the Palmers', near Willoughby's estate, and Marianne becomes seriously ill. Willoughby, hearing of her illness, comes seeking forgiveness. He bares his soul to Elinor, pouring out his regrets and giving some explanation for his behavior to Marianne and to Colonel Brandon's young ward. His wealthy aunt, who controlled his fortune, cut him off when hearing of his sordid affair, and the "dread of poverty" led him to marry the ill-mannered Miss Grey.

After some harrowing nights, Marianne begins to recover, and the sisters return to domestic stability with their mother in Barton Cottage. Marianne, learning what Willoughby has told Elinor, slowly ceases to believe that he was her one and only love. Elinor, despite her stoicism, is deeply hurt when she hears of Lucy's marriage to "Mr. Ferrars." In a less than credible plot twist, however, the conniving Lucy turns out to have married *Robert* Ferrars, shifting her affections from Edward to his brother. Free of Lucy at last, Edward comes to Barton Cottage, proposes to Elinor, and their future happiness is assured. As the book ends, Elinor, married to Edward and living in the rectory on Colonel Brandon's estate, brings her sister and Colonel Brandon together. Marianne learns the errors of her earlier behavior and beliefs, and finds comfort and happiness.

The unscrupulous Lucy and Robert remain unpunished, succeeding in making up to Mrs. Ferrars and securing their fortune. Austen's characteristic irony is clear:

> The whole of Lucy's behavior in the affair, and the prosperity which crowned it, therefore, may be held forth as a most encouraging instance of what an earnest, an unceasing attention to self-interest, however its progress may be apparently obstructed, will do in securing every advantage of fortune, with no other sacrifice than that of time and conscience.

Without belaboring the point, Austen nonetheless stresses that those who are not selfish, who suffer patiently in good conscience and struggle to reconcile the claims of head and heart, also receive their rewards. ❀

List of Characters in
Sense and Sensibility

Elinor Dashwood, the oldest of the three Dashwood sisters, possesses exemplary strength of understanding and coolness of judgment. "She had an excellent heart; her disposition was affectionate, and her feelings were strong; but she knew how to govern them," Austen writes. Reserved and practical, aware of a strong sense of duty, she is deeply devoted to her family even as their interests require her to squelch her own feelings. Beneath her composure, however, she feels passion and deep sadness. As she explains to Marianne, who accuses her of being "cold-hearted," her feelings must be gauged with respect to her self-command: "Believe them to be stronger than I have declared."

Marianne Dashwood, Elinor's younger sister, is "eager in everything; her sorrows, her joys, could have no moderation. She was generous, amiable, interesting: she was everything but prudent." Her beauty is enlivened by "a life, a spirit, an eagerness which could hardly be seen without delight," so that "when in the common cant of praise she was called a beautiful girl, truth less violently outraged than usually happens." Naïve and outspoken, Marianne exemplifies the personality ruled by "sensibility," a romantic faith in the worth of her emotions, even if their expression requires her to err against decorum. She falls hopelessly in love with John Willoughby, believing with her "natural ardour of mind" that she knows him completely.

Edward Ferrars, the brother of Elinor's sister-in-law Fanny, wins Elinor's affections with his sincerity and quiet warmth. "He was not handsome, and his manners required intimacy to make them pleasing. He was too diffident to do justice to himself; but when his natural shyness was overcome, his behaviour gave every indication of an open affectionate heart." His family wants him to be a "great man" with a prestigious career, but he would prefer "domestic comfort and the quiet of private life" as a clergyman. He honorably stands by his youthful engagement to Lucy Steele, despite his strong feelings for Elinor.

Colonel Brandon, the Middleton's wealthy neighbor, admires Marianne. He is gentlemanly but "silent and grave," dignified but rather dull. Marianne believes that he is "an absolute old bachelor, for he was on the wrong side of five and thirty" and wears flannel waistcoats for fear of catching cold. When she recovers from her infatuation with Willoughby, she overcomes her distaste and learns to value Colonel Brandon's generosity, kindness, and good sense, eventually marrying him.

John Willoughby, the dashing romantic hero who becomes the novel's villain, is gallant, impetuous, and candid. Marianne admires his "manly beauty and more than common gracefulness," his personality that "united frankness and vivacity," and his taste in poetry and music. Austen portrays Willoughby as having more depth than the usual rake of eighteenth-century fiction. He, like Marianne, has intense feelings, and we believe in the end that he regrets losing her. He is mostly concerned with his own self-interests, however, and his vanity, greed, and libertine habits decide his fate—a loveless marriage but an ample fortune and a life of leisure.

Mrs. Jennings, Lady Middleton's mother, is a great comic character, a "good humoured, merry, fat, elderly woman, who talked a great deal, seemed very happy and rather vulgar." She teases everyone mercilessly, saying "witty things on the subject of lovers and husbands." Despite her blundering, she proves to be a true advocate of the Dashwood sisters, and they appreciate her big-heartedness and caring. ❀

Critical Views on
Sense and Sensibility

[Henry James (1843–1916), one of the most esteemed and influential of all American novelists, is the author of *The Portrait of a Lady, The Wings of the Dove,* and *The Ambassadors,* among other novels. He is noted for his subtle and complex characterization and his treatment of intersections of European and American culture. He was an important critic of the novel as well. Here, James describes Austen's skill and artistry as instinctive or "unconscious," even accidental. Despite this assessment and his wryness about the commercial efforts that have helped make Austen so popular, James elegantly praises her ability to cause many readers to "lose their hearts."]

Jane Austen, with all her light felicity, leaves us hardly more curious of her process, or of the experience in her that fed it, than the brown thrush who tells his story from the garden bough; and this, I freely confess, in spite of her being one of those of the shelved and safe, for all time, of whom I should have liked to begin by talking; one of those in whose favour discrimination had long since practically operated. She is in fact a signal instance of the way it does, with all its embarrassments, at last infallibly operate. A sharp short cut, one of the sharpest and shortest achieved, in this field, by the general judgment, came out, betimes, straight at her feet. Practically overlooked for thirty or forty years after her death, she perhaps really stands there for us as the prettiest possible example of that rectification of estimate, brought about by some slow clearance of stupidity, the half-century or so is capable of working round to. This tide has risen high on the opposite shore, the shore of appreciation—risen rather higher, I think, than the high-water mark, the highest, of her intrinsic merit and interest; though I grant indeed—as a point to be made—that we are dealing here in some degree with the tides so freely driven up, beyond their mere logical reach, by the stiff breeze of the commercial, in other words of the special bookselling spirit; an eager, active, interfering force which has a great many confusions of apparent value, a great many wild and wandering estimates, to answer for. For these distinctively mechanical and overdone reactions, of course, the critical spirit, even in its most relaxed mood, is not responsible. Responsible, rather, is the body of publishers, editors, illustrators, producers of the pleasant twaddle of magazines; who have found their "dear", our dear, everybody's dear, Jane so infinitely to their material purpose, so amenable to pretty reproduction in every variety of what is called tasteful, and in what seemingly proves to be saleable, form.

I do not, naturally, mean that she would be saleable if we had not more or less—beginning with Macaulay, her first slightly ponderous amoroso—lost our hearts to her; but I cannot help seeing her, a good deal, as in the same lucky box as the Brontës—lucky for the ultimate guerdon; a case of popularity (that in especial of the Yorkshire sisters), a beguiled infatuation, a sentimentalized vision, determined largely by the accidents and circumstances originally surrounding the manifestation of the genius—only with the reasons for the sentiment, in this latter connection, turned the other way. The key to Jane Austen's fortune with posterity has been in part the extraordinary grace of her facility, in fact of her unconsciousness: as if, at the most, for difficulty, for embarrassment, she sometimes, over her work basket, her tapestry flowers, in the spare, cool drawing-room of other days, fell a-musing, lapsed too metaphorically, as one may say, into wool-gathering, and her dropped stitches, of these pardonable, of these precious moments, were afterwards picked up as little touches of human truth, little glimpses of steady vision, little master-strokes of imagination.

—Henry James, "The Lesson of Balzac (1905)." In *The House of Fiction* (London: Rupert Hart-Davis, 1957): pp. 62–63.

A. WALTON LITZ ON CHARACTER TYPES

[A. Walton Litz is Holmes Professor of English at
Princeton University and the author of several books of
criticism, including important studies of James Joyce,
William Carlos Williams, Wallace Stevens, T. S. Eliot, and
Ezra Pound. In this extract, Litz describes Austen's effort
to transform the literary stereotypes of moralistic fiction,
in which characters represent antithetical temperaments,
but he concludes that Austen had not yet succeeded in
moving beyond this convention.]

The titles *Sense and Sensibility* and *Pride and Prejudice* derive
from a standard thematic pattern set by late eighteenth-century
moralistic fiction, in which opposed qualities of mind are
dramatized through opposed personalities, usually sisters or close
friends of radically different temperaments. Of course Jane Austen
sought to modify this antithetical structure in creating *Sense and
Sensibility,* and she transformed it almost beyond recognition
in the final version of *Pride and Prejudice,* where it would be
difficult to associate the hero with one particular quality and
the heroine with its opposite. But the rigid antithetical form was
her starting point in both novels, and in *Sense and Sensibility*
she never escaped from it; we are still justified in saying that
Marianne represents Sensibility while Elinor stands for Sense. In
Sense and Sensibility we witness that struggle between an inher-
ited form and fresh experience which so often marks the transi-
tional works of a great artist. ⟨. . .⟩

Marvin Mudrick had advanced the theory that Jane Austen,
having abandoned the ironic attacks on excessive sensibility found
in the *Juvenilia,* resorted in *Sense and Sensibility* to the self-defeating
device of smothering feeling under dead social conventions. He
makes the shrewd observations that Elinor, for all her Sense, has
hardly been a better judge of Willoughby's character than Marianne;
that her prudence is really a shrinking from commitment; and that
Jane Austen's final exaltation of Elinor's judgment over Marianne's
feeling is a falsification of the novel's action. Having demonstrated
that the events of the novel do not confirm its ostensible theme,
the superiority of Sense to Sensibility, Mudrick then concludes that
in *Sense and Sensibility* Jane Austen turned from her youthful attacks
on the false sensibility to an attack on all feeling. "Feeling is bad

because it is a personal commitment," and Jane Austen, trapped in a world where the only alternative to Willoughby is Colonel Brandon, finds her only solace in detachment. She defends herself against this world not with irony, as in her earlier works, but with the lifeless facade of socially accepted attitudes.

This is in many ways a tempting view, but I cannot square it with the general pattern of Jane Austen's development or with the obvious attempts in *Sense and Sensibility* to mediate between reason and feeling, social conventions and individual passion. The alternative to Willoughby is Colonel Brandon *not* because this was Jane Austen's heritage from life, but because it was her heritage from the broad antitheses of moralistic fiction. Similarly, Marianne's sensibility is continually degenerating into excess, and Elinor's common-sense into lifeless decorum, because it was the nature of the contemporary novel's form and language to sharpen, rather than lessen, antitheses. Jane Austen's lack of enthusiasm for these schematic oppositions is evident in the hackneyed tale with which Colonel Brandon explains Willoughby's character. The sincerity and passion of Willoughby's final confession to Elinor indicate the direction of the author's ambitions, but this fine scene is ultimately negated by the reversion to literary stereotypes in the final chapter.

The depressing atmosphere which hangs over so much of *Sense and Sensibility* can, in short, be attributed to the fact that Jane Austen was working against her natural inclinations and talents. She was the victim of conventions, but these were primarily artistic, not social. The brilliant ironic effects of her earlier fiction had been local ones, and she was not able in her revisions of *Sense and Sensibility* to evolve a structure that could sustain her ironic vision. It was only with *Pride and Prejudice*, where the revisions struck much deeper, that she put her criticism of contemporary fiction to full use and achieved a form that we recognize as uniquely her own.

—A. Walton Litz, *Jane Austen: A Study of Her Artistic Development* (New York: Oxford University Press, 1965): pp. 73–83.

[Norman Page is professor of English at the University of Alberta and the author of *The Language of Jane Austen,* *Speech in the English Novel,* and several other critical works. In this extract, Page examines the use of interpolated letters and references to letters throughout the novel. Remnants of the novel's earlier epistolary form, these letters function to further the plot, demonstrate social relationships, and develop dramatic tension.]

Later in the 1790s, Jane Austen initiated a more ambitious phase of her career with the writing, probably some time before 1796, of the epistolary novel *Elinor and Marianne.* Since this has not survived, we can only conjecture its nature by working backwards from the published novel that represents a radical rewriting of this earlier work, and such conjectures must of necessity be imperfect and incomplete. The abandonment of the epistolary form in *Sense and Sensibility* may be interpreted as an unmistakable symptom of the author's dissatisfaction with it; yet the rejection was not complete, and (as B. C. Southam has pointed out) certain passages of the final novel, and some of its structural and narrative devices, betray the nature of the original design. An examination of the role of letters in this novel will reveal the extent of its relationship to the epistolary method.

Letters make their appearance in *Sense and Sensibility* in a number of ways, ranging from brief allusions to the quotation *verbatim* of an entire letter occupying several pages, and from passing references to letter-writing as an activity to the sending and receipt of letters which play a vital part in the story. A letter can be a useful plot-device, its purpose extending no further than the contrivance of some necessary piece of action; of this kind is the letter received by Mrs. Dashwood in the fourth chapter. She is offered a cottage in Devon, and promptly sends her acceptance, after showing the letter she has written to her two daughters. More important than this is the letter which is used to show character and relationships; since the strict code of conventions governed the sending and receiving of letters by eligible but unmarried persons of different sexes, the mere possession of a letter became a certificate of intimacy. This convention is invoked when Lucy Steele shows Elinor the letter she has received from Edward Ferrars, thereby disclosing her engagement to him. Most important of all, however, is the use of a letter as the centre of a dramatic situation, and here the most memorable of many examples is the scene in which Elinor finds the prostrate Marianne, "almost choked with grief", clutching a letter in her hand and with three others scattered around her—the cause of this emotional crisis being the receipt of a cold and formal note from Willoughby.

As one examines the many references to epistolary activity in this novel, it becomes clear that two main correspondences are involved, together with a number of minor ones of slighter interest. One is the partly clandestine correspondence between Marianne and Willoughby, the other the frequent exchange of letters between Mrs. Dashwood in Devon and her daughters in London, since the latter are separated from their mother for a large portion of the action. ⟨. . .⟩

Through the greater part of the novel, therefore, letters written, received or awaited play an important part in the development of the action and occupy the stage in a number of episodes. And, to anticipate a point that will be returned to later in this chapter, there is a congruity between letter-writing styles and their authors: Marianne's to Willoughby are "full of affection and confidence", his is "impudently cruel", and Lucy Steele's give Mrs. Jennings pleasure ("how prettily she writes!") but cause Edward only mortification.

—Norman Page, *The Language of Jane Austen* (New York: Harper & Row Publishers, Barnes & Noble Division, 1972): pp. 174–177.

CLAUDIA JOHNSON ON SOCIAL CRITIQUE

[Claudia Johnson is professor of English at Princeton University and the author of *Equivocal Beings: Politics, Gender, and Sentimentality in the 1790s* and *Jane Austen: Women, Politics, and the Novel*, from which this excerpt is taken. Johnson argues that *Sense and Sensibility* is "unremitting in its cynicism and iconoclasm."]

Well before the establishment of "the subversive school" in Austenian criticism, Austen's more acute admirers perceived what

Margaret Oliphant called her "fine vein of feminine cynicism" about the worldliness around her, and Reginald Farrer considered such cynicism so radical that he called Jane Austen "the most merciless, though calmest, of iconoclasts." Charges of cynicism and iconoclasm particularly befit *Sense and Sensibility*, for this dark and disenchanted novel exposes how those sacred and supposedly benevolizing institutions of order—property, marriage, and family—actually enforce avarice, shiftlessness, and oppressive mediocrity. In *Sense and Sensibility* there are no dependable normative centers—no sane Gardiners or hale Crofts who serve as havens from the fatuity and vitiation rampant elsewhere. Edward Ferrars certainly cannot serve in this capacity, for his own derelictions are a part of the problem. And the other eligible figure, Colonel Brandon, refuses the voice of moral censor. Anticipating his concurrence, Elinor laments that Marianne's "systems" set "propriety at nought." But Brandon, unlike Elinor herself, had had that "better acquaintance with the world" which Elinor would prescribe to Marianne. Knowledge of the world has only made him value the "romantic refinements of a young mind" such as Marianne's all the more, and regret that those "opinions" that pass as proper in the world are "too common, and too dangerous." Well might Brandon cherish Marianne's defiance of worldly commonplaces, since the world of *Sense and Sensibility* harbors such moral nullities as John Dashwood, who is "well-respected" precisely because "he conducted himself with propriety," and Lady Middleton, that exemplar of decorum, who instinctively hates the superiority of the Dashwood sisters: "because they were fond of reading, she fancied them satirical: perhaps without exactly knowing what it was to be satirical; but *that* did not signify. It was censure in common use, and easily given."

Of all Austen's novels, *Sense and Sensibility* is the most attuned to progressive social criticism. Like their counterparts in the political fiction of the 1790s, when "Elinor and Marianne" was drafted, the characters here are exceptionally conscious of how ideology, that only apparently natural system of priorities, practices, and attitudes, delimits all our social behavior, and the novel as a whole assails the dominant ideology of its time for privileging the greedy, mean-spirited, and pedestrian. *Sense and Sensibility* is not, as it is often assumed to be, a dramatized conduct book partly favoring female prudence over female impetuosity, as if those qualities could be discussed apart from the larger world of politics. Indeed, it is only because that larger world around them is so menacing in the first place that the manners of young ladies are of such consequence. Provided she appear proper and play the sycophant to wealth and power, a cold-hearted heroine like Lucy Steele finds a place in the world. But for romantic heroines like Elinor and Marianne, who in their own ways challenge the commonplace, the scenario reads quite differently. Whereas conduct books teach young women the social codes they must adopt if they are to live acceptably as wives and daughters, fully integrated into their communities, *Sense and Sensibility* makes those codes and the communities that dictate them the subject of its interrogation, and what is at stake finally is not propriety, but survival. While it has seemed to virtually all readers that Marianne's very independence from the dominant mores of her society subjects her to Austen's satire, in many ways the case is just the opposite. In this novel, the destiny assigned to romantic heroines is betrayal—and this at the hands of "respectable" country gentlemen. If Marianne has resisted the codes which not only require but reward calculation and coldheartedness, she has submitted without resistance to those which dictate desolation and very nearly death as the price of feeling.

—Claudia Johnson, *Jane Austen: Women, Politics, and the Novel* (Chicago: University of Chicago Press, 1988): pp. 49–50.

NORA NACHUMI ON FILM ADAPTATION

[Nora Nachumi is completing a Ph.D. at the City University of New York and is the recipient of a fellowship from the American Association of University Women. Nachumi argues that the sexy actors and sentimental images in Emma Thompson's 1995 movie *Sense and Sensibility* convey a very different attitude toward romance than Austen's novel does.]

Written by Emma Thompson and directed by Ang Lee, the 1995 movie version of *Sense and Sensibility* actually celebrates the conventions of romance the novel condemns. The book ends as it begins, by foregrounding the relationship of Elinor and Marianne. The movie concludes with the marriage of Colonel Brandon and Marianne and—in direct opposition to the novel—emphasizes Willoughby's sorrow. The book tells us that Willoughby "lived to exert, and frequently to enjoy himself." The screenplay, however, ends with Willoughby on a white horse, *"on the far edge of [the] frame,"* watching as Brandon tosses coins into the air. *"As we draw back further still,"* the screenplay concludes, *"he slowly pulls the horse around and moves off in the opposite direction."*

Willoughby's white horse, and horses in general, are a key to the movie version of *Sense and Sensibility*. That Willoughby rides the white horse of a hero suggests that Emma Thompson clearly understands Austen's intentions regarding the disparity between the way Willoughby looks and behaves (a stage direction when Willoughby leaves Barton Cottage describes him as *"looking about as virile as his horse"*). However, the fact that Brandon's black charger is equally, if more subtly, virile points to a crucial difference between the novel and the film. Despite a few reservations, Thompson's screenplay intentionally glorifies the romantic conventions that Austen deflates. In her published diary, Thompson remarks that "making the male characters effective was one of the biggest problems" in translating the novel to film. "In the novel," she remarks, "Edward and Brandon are quite shadowy and absent for long periods." In a movie that ends up celebrating romance, this is a serious problem.

Thompson's solution was to "keep [the men] present even when they're off screen." One way this was accomplished was in the casting. Austen's Edward Ferrars is not a hunk. He "was not recommended to [the Dashwoods] by any peculiar graces of person or address" remarks the narrator. "He was not handsome, and his manners required intimacy to make them pleasing." In the movie, Edward is played by Hugh Grant, a man Thompson describes as "Repellently gorgeous . . . much prettier than I am." Although he is not precisely pretty, Alan Rickman as Brandon is definitely more macho than someone who is described as wearing flannel waistcoats has a right to be. He frequently is filmed with a gun or a horse, and his disheveled appearance as Marianne lies ill out-Byrons Willoughby. "Give me an occupation," he murmurs to Elinor, "or I shall run mad." After this, the screenplay asserts, he is *"dangerously quiet."* This is much more exciting than Austen's description of a man who, "with a readiness that seemed to speak the occasion, and the service pre-arranged in his mind . . . offered himself as the messenger who should fetch Mrs. Dashwood." Clearly Brandon, as played by Rickman, is far sexier than Austen intended him to be.

Indeed, the movie works hard to create the impression that Brandon is the perfect romantic hero for Marianne. Specifically, Thompson's screenplay revises the novel so that Brandon's later actions mirror Willoughby's earlier behavior. In the movie, both carry an incapacitated Marianne through the rain. Both ride powerful chargers, and both recite poetry to her with heartfelt conviction. Brandon even concludes his poetry reading with what the screenplay describes as a *"soul-breathing glance."* Austen, in contrast, is notoriously reluctant to describe love scenes of any kind. In the novel, the courtship of Marianne and Colonel Brandon is described thus: "With such a confederacy against her—with a knowledge so intimate of his goodness—with a conviction of his fond attachment to herself, which at last, though long after it was observable to everybody else—burst on her— what could she do?" Thompson's movie works, but, ironically, it works by celebrating the very tropes Austen destabilizes.

—Nora Nachumi, "'As If!': Translating Austen's Ironic Narrator to Film." In *Jane Austen in Hollywood,* eds. Linda Troost and Sayre Greenfield (Lexington: University Press of Kentucky, 1998): pp. 132–133.

Plot Summary of
Pride and Prejudice

The novel begins with one of the most famous first lines in literature: "It is a truth universally acknowledged that a single man in possession of a good fortune must be in want of a wife." Belief in this "truth" is upheld with particular urgency by Mrs. Bennet, who has five daughters without dowries to marry off. Lacking a male heir, Mr. Bennet must leave his property to their ridiculous and obsequious cousin, Mr. Collins, while his daughters negotiate their own places in society, forming attachments and suffering disappointments as their different merits and flaws allow. The most popular of Austen's novels, *Pride and Prejudice* examines marriage and manners in Regency England through vibrant characterization and comic aplomb.

Volume I opens with the announcement that a wealthy eligible bachelor, Mr. Bingley, has leased nearby Netherfield. Mrs. Bennet immediately hopes that one of her daughters will marry him. The two eldest, Jane and Elizabeth, are elegant, beautiful, and intelligent. Elizabeth, the novel's central character, is witty and high-spirited; she is her father's favorite. The younger daughters are less respectable. The homely and bookish Mary lacks intelligence but compensates with a "pedantic air and conceited manner." Kitty and Lydia, "vain, ignorant, idle and absolutely uncontrolled," are prone to giddy and frivolous behavior: "while there was an officer in Meryton, they would flirt with him."

At a local ball, the Bennets meet Mr. Bingley and his friend Mr. Darcy, an extremely wealthy and attractive gentleman who is "discovered to be proud, to be above his company, and above being pleased." Mr. Bingley is struck by Jane's beauty and quickly appears partial to her. Mr. Darcy snubs Elizabeth, within earshot, as "tolerable; but not handsome enough to tempt me." Offended, but enough at ease with herself to laugh about it, Elizabeth discusses his haughty manners with her sister and Charlotte Lucas, her close friend. At subsequent gatherings, Mr. Darcy takes further notice of Elizabeth, who responds coolly and saucily.

Jane is befriended by Mr. Bingley's "proud and conceited" sisters and is invited to visit Netherfield. Caught in the rain, she comes down with a cold and must stay there. Elizabeth, out of affection for her sister, refuses to stand on ceremony and hurries over to take care of her. Spending an awkward week with the Bingleys while Jane gets well, Elizabeth converses reluctantly with Mr. Darcy and endures Miss Bingley's snobbishness. Mrs. Bennet arrives and makes a scene with the younger sisters, much to Elizabeth's embarrassment. Mr. Darcy now realizes that he "had never been so bewitched by any woman as he was by her. He really believed that were it not for the inferiority of her connections he should be in some danger."

Mr. Collins, Mr. Bennet's irksome heir, pays a visit, intending to choose one of the Bennet daughters as a wife to make amends for inheriting the Bennet property. A clergyman on the estate of Lady Catherine de Bourgh, Mr. Collins talks incessantly about his rich patroness, who is also Mr. Darcy's aunt. At this time, the Bennet sisters meet new officers in Meryton. The amiable and good-looking George Wickham captivates Elizabeth's attention, and confides in her about the injustice he has suffered at Mr. Darcy's hands. Wickham claims that Darcy has denied him a living as a clergyman on his estate, Pemberley, which had been promised to him by Darcy's father, Wickham's godfather. Hearing of Mr. Darcy's unfairness, Elizabeth, already less than fond of him, forms a deep prejudice, completing the antagonism between the two principal characters that Austen outlines in the book's title.

The contentious attraction between Mr. Darcy and Elizabeth is further developed at the Netherfield ball, where they engage in feisty conversation. The next day, Mr. Collins, warned that Jane is being courted by Mr. Bingley, dutifully proposes to the next sister in line, Elizabeth, condescendingly reminding her how grateful she should be. She emphatically refuses, to her mother's dismay (and her father's relief). Undaunted, Mr. Collins promptly proposes to the practical Charlotte Lucas, who accepts. Elizabeth is disappointed that her friend is willing to marry such an intolerable man, but recognizes sadly that marriage and mutual affection do not necessarily coincide. Though Jane and Mr. Bingley clearly like each other, Jane is disappointed to find out that the Bingleys are leaving abruptly for London. Miss Bingley insinuates that her brother is courting Darcy's younger sister, Georgiana.

In **Volume II,** Jane goes to London to visit her respectable and kind aunt and uncle, the Gardiners. She reports, unhappily, that

Miss Bingley has been cold toward her and that she has not seen Mr. Bingley at all. Even the good-natured Jane, who was at first sure that Miss Bingley was "incapable of willfully deceiving any one," is forced to admit "there is a strong appearance of duplicity in all this." Elizabeth also leaves the Bennet home in Longbourn for an extended visit with Charlotte and Mr. Collins, where she meets Darcy's aunt, the bossy and condescending Lady Catherine de Bourgh, who is fond of "dictating to others" and must be continually appeased with "excessive admiration."

Mr. Darcy also pays a visit to Lady Catherine, his aunt, and he and Elizabeth continue to meet. She is deeply shocked when, in a highly charged scene, Darcy proposes to her, telling her that his love has enabled him to overcome his distaste for her relatives. She is insulted and lashes out with the accusation that he has ruined her sister's prospects with Mr. Bingley and cheated Wickham. Mr. Darcy leaves hastily, but the next day writes a letter that clears up some misperceptions. He admits that he interfered to prevent Bingley from marrying Jane, but Wickham himself had given up claim to the living Darcy's father had promised, in exchange for a substantial sum of money, which he soon squandered. Moreover, he was prone to chasing heiresses and had tried to seduce Mr. Darcy's young sister. Realizing Wickham's deceit, but still angry that Mr. Darcy insulted her family and hurt Jane, Elizabeth allows only some of her prejudice to dissolve.

Elizabeth returns to Longbourn, where Lydia, despite Elizabeth's vehement objections about "such double danger as a watering place and a camp," persuades her parents to allow her to go to Brighton. Lydia's "restless ecstasy" forebodes trouble. In **Volume III,** Elizabeth departs with the Gardiners on a summer vacation that takes them into Derbyshire, where they take a tour of Pemberley, Mr. Darcy's beautiful estate. Elizabeth is embarrassed when she finds Mr. Darcy unexpectedly at home, and is surprised by his gracious hospitality toward her relatives. He even introduces Elizabeth to his sister and displays such warm regard that Elizabeth begins to believe that she has not completely alienated him. Her feelings toward him soften further, but before she can understand his changed behavior, she receives bad news: Lydia has eloped with Wickham. Elizabeth, now knowing what she does of Wickham's character, realizes that he has no intention of really marrying her, and fears that her sister is permanently disgraced. Mr. Darcy witnesses her great distress.

Returning home quickly, Elizabeth finds her family in upheaval. After several weeks of suspense, they hear that Lydia and Wickham have been discovered and persuaded to marry, but only after Wickham is monetarily coerced, presumably at Mr. Gardiner's expense. Lydia, oblivious to the pain she has caused and the ruin she has skirted, comes home triumphant and is welcomed warmly by Mrs. Bennet, who thinks only of her success in having a daughter married at last. Elizabeth discovers that Mr. Darcy put up the money to rescue her sister. Perplexed and grateful, she realizes finally that she loves him, but believes she has lost him irrevocably due to the shame of her family's recent crisis.

With Mr. Darcy's pride diminished and Elizabeth's prejudice quelled, however, the major obstacles to the happiness of the principal characters have been removed. Mr. Bingley, encouraged and accompanied by Mr. Darcy, reappears in the neighborhood and resumes his attentions to Jane. He soon proposes. Lady Catherine arrives unexpectedly and sternly reprimands Elizabeth: rumors have circulated that Mr. Darcy intends to marry her, and Lady Catherine declares that he is intended for her daughter, trying to extort a promise that Elizabeth will refuse him if he asks. With characteristic poise and spunk, she refuses to be bullied.

In a poignant scene, Mr. Darcy tells Elizabeth that his love for her remains unchanged. She replies that "her sentiments had undergone so material a change . . . as to make her receive with gratitude and pleasure his present assurances." Their happiness is palpable, and the news of their engagement is conveyed to her incredulous family. Ending with the promise of two happy marriages, assured by Mr. Bingley and Jane's easy compatibility, and Mr. Darcy and Elizabeth's playful rapport, *Pride and Prejudice* is optimistic about marriage and about harmony among different social groups. ❀

List of Characters in
Pride and Prejudice

About protagonist **Elizabeth Bennet,** Austen remarked, "I must confess that I think her as delightful a creature as ever appeared in print," and her opinion has been shared by many readers. Vivacious, intelligent, confident, Elizabeth is admirable for her spirited determination. Though she is not quite as beautiful as her older sister, her face is "rendered uncommonly intelligent by the beautiful expression of her dark eyes." She is frank, sometimes argumentative, and fond of analyzing the inconsistencies of people's characters. Her own motives are not always clear to her, but she comes to greater self-awareness as the story unfolds. After Mr. Darcy's first proposal, she berates herself for being "blind, partial, prejudiced, absurd" and wishes for a chance to redress her unjust accusations. She is self-reflective, ashamed that she "meant to be uncommonly clever in taking so decided a dislike to him, without any reason." Through her sincerity, capacity for change, and strong sense of self-worth, she attains equal, passionate love.

Fitzwilliam Darcy, aloof and self-assured, is disliked by Elizabeth for his snobbish demeanor. He is distinguished by a "fine, tall person, handsome features, noble mien—and the report which was in general circulation within five minutes after his entrance of his having ten thousand a year." Perceived through Elizabeth's eyes, he is "haughty, reserved, and fastidious, and his manners, though well bred, were not inviting," but our opinion of him changes as Elizabeth's does. When her dislike is at its height, she rejects him for his "arrogance" and "selfish disdain of the feelings of others," but we find, to the contrary, that he is generous, concerned, and impartial. He is a devoted guardian to his sister, a loyal friend, and an honorable and conscientious landlord. Like Elizabeth, he is capable of change, and even his most deeply ingrained pride is weakened by love. What he once saw as her impertinence and impropriety, he comes to sees as the "liveliness of [her] mind," and at the novel's end he and Elizabeth become engaged.

Jane Bennet, Elizabeth's older sister, is "candid without ostentation or design," and incapable of thinking ill of anyone. Her openness sometimes shades into naïveté, and she is the last to know that she is being deceived, but her good nature cannot be marred: "Jane united with great strength of feeling a composure of temper and a uniform cheerfulness of manner." She is in love with, and eventually becomes engaged to, Mr. Bingley.

Charles Bingley, like Jane, is contented by nature, and known for the "easiness, openness, ductility of his temper." He is a little too easily swayed by the opinions of others, and gives in to his sisters' petulance and Mr. Darcy's snobbery. He allows himself to be convinced that Jane, whom Mr. Darcy thinks is beneath his serious notice, does not love him. When the obstacles are removed, however, their courtship is swift and uneventful, to the mutual happiness of both.

Mrs. Bennet is, as Margaret Drabble writes in her introduction to *Pride and Prejudice,* "vulgar, impossible, stupid, uncultured, [and] embarrassing." She is "a woman of mean understanding, little information, and uncertain temper. . . . The business of her life was to get her daughters married; its solace was visiting and news."

Mr. Bennet is an odd mixture of "sarcastic humour, reserve, and caprice." Married to a woman he does not respect, he observes her folly and that of his younger daughters with amusement and with no effort to curb their frivolous behavior.

Mr. Collins, the cousin who is heir to the Bennet estate, is a hopelessly long-winded clergyman, a "conceited, pompous, narrow-minded, silly man," "a mixture of pride and obsequiousness, self-importance and humility." He unsuccessfully courts the two eldest Bennet sisters, then proposes to Elizabeth's friend, Charlotte Lucas.

Lady Catherine de Bourgh is the bossy and nosy "eminent personage" in the novel. As Austen sardonically explains, "she was not rendered formidable by silence; but whatever she said was spoken in so authoritative a tone as marked her self-importance." A "tall, large woman" with a tiny, sickly daughter, she demands obsequious attention: "there was little to be done but to hear Lady Catherine talk, which she did without any intermission till coffee came in, delivering her opinion on every subject in so decisive a manner as proved that she was not used to have her judgment controverted." ❀

Critical Views on
Pride and Prejudice

AUSTEN COMMENTS ON THE NOVEL

[In these excerpts from letters to her sister Cassandra, Austen expresses delight in seeing the published copies of *Pride and Prejudice* but offers a few self-critical views of her own. Few readers have objected to the "light, and bright, and sparkling" quality of this most popular of all her novels, which she herself called "my own darling child," and fewer still would want her to include "the history of Buonaparté" to make it more somber, but these half-serious remarks nonetheless suggest her goals for her next book, *Mansfield Park*.]

Chawton, Friday Jan 29

To Cassandra Austen,

Miss Benn dined with us on the very day of the books coming & in the evening we set fairly at it, and read half the first vol. to her, prefacing that, having intelligence from Henry that such a work would soon appear, we had desired him to send it whenever it came out, and I believe it passed with her unsuspected. She was amused, poor soul! *That* she could not help, you know, with two such people to lead the way, but she really does seem to admire Elizabeth. I must confess that I think her as delightful a creature as ever appeared in print, and how I shall be able to tolerate those who do not like *her* at least I do not know. There are a few typical errors; and a 'said he,' or a 'said she,' would sometimes make the dialogue more immediately clear; but

> I do not write for such dull elves
> As have not a great deal of ingenuity themselves.

Chawton, Thursday Feb 4

My dear Cassandra,

Your letter was truly welcome, and I am much obliged to you all for your praise; it came at a right time, for I had had some fits of disgust. Our second evening's reading to Miss Benn had not pleased me so well, but I believe something must be attributed to my mother's too rapid way of getting on: and though she perfectly understands the characters herself, she cannot speak as they ought. Upon the whole, however, I am quite vain enough and well satisfied enough. The work is rather too light, and bright, and sparkling; it wants shade; it wants to be stretched out here and there with a long chapter of sense, if it could be had; if not, of solemn specious nonsense, about something unconnected with the story; an essay on writing, a critique on Walter Scott, or the history of Buonaparté, or anything that would form a contrast, and bring the reader with increased delight to the playfulness and epigrammatism of the general style. I doubt your quite agreeing with me here. I know your starched notions. The caution observed at Steventon with regard to the possession of the book is an agreeable surprise to me, & I heartily wish it may be the means of saving you from everything unpleasant—but you must be prepared for the neighbourhood being perhaps already informed of there being such a Work in the World & in the Chawton World!

—Jane Austen to Cassandra Austen, January 29, 1813, and February 4, 1813, in *Jane Austen's Letters to Her Sister Cassandra and Others*, ed. R. W. Chapman (New York: Oxford University Press, 1952): pp. 297–300.

AN EARLY REVIEW

[From its first publication in January 1813, *Pride and Prejudice* stood out as remarkable among the novels of its time. This anonymous reviewer remarks especially on Austen's skillful characterization and the "great spirit" of her portraits.]

We had occasion to speak favorably of the former production of this author or authoress, specified above, and we readily do the same of the present. It is very far superior to almost all the publications of the kind which have lately come before us. It has a very unexceptionable tendency, the story is well told, the characters remarkably well drawn and supported, and written with great spirit as well as vigour. The story has no great variety, it is simply this. The hero is a young man of large fortune and fashionable manners, whose distinguishing characteristic is personal pride. The heroine, on the first introduction, conceives a most violent prejudice against Darcy, which a variety of circumstances well imagined and happily represented, tend to strengthen and confirm. The under plot is an attachment between the friend of Darcy and the elder sister of the principle female character; other personages, of greater or less interest and importance, complete the dramatis personæ, some of whose characters are exceedingly well drawn. Explanations of the different perplexities and seeming contrarieties, are gradually unfolded, and the two principle performers are happily united.

Of the characters, Elizabeth Bennet, the heroine, is supported with great spirit and consistency throughout; there seems no defect in the portrait; this is not precisely the case with Darcy her lover; his easy unconcern and fashionable indifference, somewhat abruptly changes to the ardent lover. The character of Mr. Collins, the obsequious rector, is excellent. Fancy presents us with many such, who consider the patron of exalted rank as the model of all that is excellent on earth, and the patron's smiles and condescension as the sum of human happiness. Mr. Bennet, the father of Elizabeth, presents us with some novelty of character; a reserved, acute, and satirical, but indolent personage, who sees and laughs at the follies and indiscretions of his dependents, without making any exertions to correct them. The picture of the younger Miss Bennets, their perpetual visits to the market town where officers are quartered, and the result, is perhaps exemplified in every provincial town in the kingdom.

It is unnecessary to add, that we have perused these volumes with much satisfaction and amusement, and entertain very little doubt that their successful circulation will induce the author to similar exertions.

—Unsigned notice, *British Critic* (February 1813). Reprinted in *Jane Austen: The Critical Heritage, Vol. 1 (1811-1870)*, ed. B. C. Southam (New York: Routledge, 1995): pp. 41–42.

[Ian Watt is Professor of English Emeritus at Stanford University and the author of *The Rise of the Novel,* an important study of literary realism, *Myths of Modern Individualism,* and several other studies. In this excerpt, he describes Austen's novels as the culmination of several developments of eighteenth-century fiction, and describes her innovations in using the "commenting narrator."]

Fanny Burney [English novelist, 1752–1840] and Jane Austen followed Fielding in adopting a more detached attitude to their narrative material, and in evaluating it from a comic and objective point of view. It is here that Jane Austen's technical genius manifests itself. She dispensed with the participating narrator, whether as the author of a memoir as in Defoe, or as letter-writer as in Richardson, probably because both of these roles make freedom to comment and evaluate more difficult to arrange; instead she told her stories after Fielding's manner, as a confessed author. Jane Austen's variant of the commenting narrator, however, was so much more discreet that it did not substantially affect the authenticity of her narrative. Her analyses of her characters and their states of mind, and her ironical juxtaposition of motive and situation are as pointed as anything in Fielding, but they do not seem to come from an intrusive author but rather from some august and impersonal spirit of social and psychological understanding.

At the same time, Jane Austen varied her narrative point of view sufficiently to give us, not only editorial comment, but much of Defoe's and Richardson's psychological closeness to the subjective world of the characters. In her novels there is usually one character whose consciousness is tacitly accorded a privileged status, and whose mental life is rendered more completely than that of the other characters. In *Pride and Prejudice* (published 1813), for example, the story is told substantially from the point of view of Elizabeth Bennet, the heroine; but the identification is always qualified by the other role of the narrator acting as dispassionate analyst, and as a result the reader does not lose his critical awareness of the novel as a whole. The same strategy as regards point of view is employed with supreme brilliance in *Emma* (1816), a novel which combines Fielding's characteristic strength in conveying the sense of society as a whole, with something of Henry James's capacity for locating the essential structural continuity of his novel in the reader's growing awareness of the full complexity of the personality and situation of the character through whom the story is mainly told: the unfolding of Emma Woodhouse's inner being has much of the drama of progressive revelation with which James presents Maisie Farange or Lambert Strether.

Jane Austen's novels, in short, must be seen as the most successful solutions of the two general narrative problems for which Richardson and Fielding had provided only partial answers. She was able to combine into a harmonious unity the advantages both of realism of presentation and realism of assessment, of the internal and of the external approaches to character; her novels have authenticity without diffuseness or trickery, wisdom of social comment without a garrulous essayist, and a sense of the social order which is not achieved at the expense of the individuality and autonomy of the characters.

Jane Austen's novels are also the climax of many other aspects of the eighteenth-century novel. In their subjects, despite some obvious differences, they continue many of the characteristic interests of Defoe, Richardson and Fielding. Jane Austen faces more squarely than Defoe, for example, the social and moral problems raised by economic individualism and the middle-class quest for improved status; she follows Richardson in basing her novels on marriage and especially on the proper feminine role in the matter; and her ultimate picture of the proper norms of the social system is similar to that of Fielding although its application to the characters and their situation is in general more serious and discriminating.

—Ian Watt, *The Rise of the Novel* (Berkeley: University of California Press, 1957): pp. 296–297.

ALICE CHANDLER ON SEXUAL ATTRACTION

[Alice Chandler is the author of *Dream of Order: The Medieval Ideal in Nineteenth-Century English Literature.* In this excerpt, Chandler describes how Austen uses the language of wit and epigram, and body language, to reveal sexual attraction between her characters, and then describes the dance scenes as exemplifying these strategies.]

Jane Austen, then, is not so innocent as we have imagined her, nor devoid of resources for expressing what she knows. But while I think it important to demonstrate the exclusively sexual element in her novels, I have isolated these examples from their context only to prove the point that she is neither ignorant nor fearful, and certainly not prim. What is more important about Jane Austen's art, however, is the way in which she fuses the physical with the emotional and the intellectual to create a sense of total human relationships. It is a restrained art that limits its subject matter and finds its material in the commonplaces of daily activity—in speaking and smiling, in walking and dancing. But it is a translucent surface that reveals the emotions underneath. The techniques she uses and the values she prescribes can best be seen in *Pride and Prejudice*, her fullest study of male-female relationships.

In attempting to trace the course of a love affair, the French romancers of the seventeenth century had recourse to a device called the *carte du tendre*—a map which treated the progress of affection through all the pleasant territories of Inclination, Complaisance, Tenderness, and Respect and all the hostile areas of Pride, Negligence, Indiscretion, and Mischance. *Pride and Prejudice* explores much the same geography of the feelings, but never abstractly and always against the familiar background of the English landscape. Because its hero and heroine are Elizabeth and Darcy, the most articulate of all Jane Austen's protagonists, these conscious and unconscious attractions and repulsions are usually turned into language, into a surface structure of wit and epigram. But body language is also speech and, like purely verbal communication, reveals attitudes of aversion and attraction. Exemplified by gestures and actions that are at once realistic and metaphoric, the method is brilliantly revealing.

Nowhere is the combination of realism and metaphor more clearly shown than in her use of dance. It is possible to reconstruct many of the social customs of the age simply by studying the descriptions of balls and dances in *Emma*, in *Mansfield Park*, in *Pride and Prejudice*, and even in *Northanger Abbey*; but it is also possible to see the ritualized encounters of the ballrooms as indicators of social and sexual definition. What partners *may* dance with one another, what partners *do* dance with one another—what woman the man chooses, what man the woman entices or resists—the pairings and nonpairings involved all provide dramatizations of the mating process that are seldom as visible elsewhere. Given the inhibitions of early nineteenth-century customs, the dance is one of the few places where choosing is apparent and touching is allowed. Jane Austen knew precisely what she meant when she says that "to be fond of dancing [is] the first step toward falling in love."

It is not surprising, then, that the first dance at Netherfield serves to define the male protagonist. Bingley, the normative man in this novel, enjoys dancing. Lively and unreserved, he dances every dance, moving from woman to woman until he fixes his feelings on Jane. The sense of flow and ease that we associate with Bingley throughout the novel appears here very plainly; he is both socially and sexually relaxed, lacking depth and firmness perhaps, but free to give and receive affection. Darcy, by contrast, is restrained. Although he has all the attributes of an attractive male—a fine, tall person, good features, and noble bearing—he is constrained and solitary. While the others pair off in dancing couples, he walks about the room alone. He is not insensible to female beauty, as his comments about Jane Bennet prove, but he is too constricted within himself—too "fastidious" Bingley calls him—to seek a partner. Ironically, proud and intolerant as he may be, his very inaccessibility enhances his worth.

—Alice Chandler, "'A Pair of Fine Eyes': Jane Austen's Treatment of Sex," *Studies in the Novel* 7, no. 1 (Spring 1975): pp. 94–95.

MAVIS BATEY ON LANDSCAPE

[Mavis Batey is the author of *Oxford Gardens: The University's Influence on Garden History, The English Garden Tour,* and *Jane Austen and the English Landscape,* from which this extract is taken. Batey situates Austen's discussions of parks and prospects within late-eighteenth century debate about the best landscaping style for English country houses. The influence of William Gilpin, who inspired a craze for

appreciating picturesque views and varied scenery, is
evident in Austen's description of Pemberley.]

Pemberley and its beautiful grounds play an important part in the
plot of *Pride and Prejudice*. The heroine, who had been so prejudiced against Mr. Darcy on first impressions, had to be shown that
he was a man of morals and of good taste. What better than to
give him a landscape of which Gilpin [William Gilpin, pioneer of
the "picturesque movement," whose writings on English landscapes inspired a craze for appreciating novel prospects and varied
scenery], Jane Austen's "best of men", would have approved; a
landscape in character with his picturesque Derbyshire scene?
The novelist's ruse was entirely satisfactory as Elizabeth was
delighted by Pemberley; and when after several more eventful
chapters she tells her sister that she has become engaged to Mr.
Darcy, and Jane asks incredulously when this extraordinary change
of attitude had taken place, Elizabeth playfully replies: "It has
been coming on so gradually, that I hardly know when it began.
But I believe I must date it from my first seeing his beautiful
grounds at Pemberley".

When Jane Austen wrote this at the end of the eighteenth century,
a controversy was raging as to what might be termed "beautiful"
in country house landscapes. The "formal mockery of princely
gardens" with flights of terraces, cascades, fountains and parterres
had long since largely been banished in England in favour of
gardens modelled on nature; but this was beautiful nature, not
wild nature. The aim of cultivating "Beautiful Nature" in mid-
eighteenth-century grounds was best described by the Palladian
Isaac Ware in 1750: "What we propose now in Gardens is to collect
the beauties of Nature and to separate them from those rude
views in which her blemishes are seen, to bring them nearer the
eye, and to dispose them in the most pleasing order and create
an universal harmony".

Beautiful forms, such as Hogarth's serpentine line from his *Analysis
of Beauty* (1753) or Burke's definition of beauty in his *Philosophical
Enquiry into the Origin of Our Ideas of the Sublime and the Beautiful*
(1757), dominated ideas in Georgian decorative art and gardening.
Smoothness, Burke said, was "a quality so essential to beauty that I
do not recollect anything beautiful that is not smooth; . . . smooth
slopes of earth in gardens; smooth streams in the landscape, in fine

women smooth skins and in several sorts of ornamental furniture, smooth and polished surfaces". Smooth beauty in landscape produced an effect of satisfaction and agreeable relaxation.

Lancelot Brown, known as "Capability" Brown, became the professional practitioner of such beautiful, satisfying landscape with smooth lawns and slopes, serpentine rivers, clumps of trees and open views. Horace Walpole thought that when Brown's Petworth Park gained "venerable maturity" it would show everything that the eighteenth century set out to achieve in "modern gardening". Jane Austen would have seen many engravings of Brown landscapes in books of gentlemen's seats and probably knew Highclere, laid out by Brown in 1770, not far from Steventon.

Samuel Richardson's *Sir Charles Grandison*, from which Jane Austen dramatised scenes for family performance, gives a typical Brown layout to Grandison Hall and so reflects the hero's aristocratic standards at a time when morals and taste were linked. The "gardens and lawns seen from the windows of the spacious house" were "as boundless as the mind of the owner and as free and open as his countenance". Grandison Hall had the essential Brown feature of a sunk fence or ha-ha so that "the eye is carried to views that have no bounds". Although Sir Charles was her paragon of virtue and Jane Austen's family recalled that "all that was ever said or done in the cedar parlour" of Grandison Hall was remembered by her, Sir Charles's views on landscaping were forty years out of date; Mr. Darcy needed a different style of landscape to show off his "Taste and Feeling" and it was to Gilpin that Jane Austen turned for guidance on the layout of Pemberley.

For Elizabeth Bennet "beautiful grounds" did not signify Burkean ideals of abstract beauty. Pemberley's attraction was Gilpin's picturesque beauty, where nature's "rude views" were not rejected and the characteristic abruptness of the Derbyshire scene was preferred to smoothness and "gradual deviations". Elizabeth felt that "she had never seen a place for which nature had done more"; this was not the gracefully elegant nature of "Capability" Brown or Grandison Hall but the nature that William Gilpin had taught Jane Austen's generation to seek out and admire with a picturesque eye.

—Mavis Batey, *Jane Austen and the English Landscape* (London: Barn Elms, 1996): pp. 68–69.

Plot Summary of
Mansfield Park

The first of Austen's "second trilogy," *Mansfield Park* is a significant departure in mood and message from *Pride and Prejudice*. Less ironic and witty, more moralistic and somber, it is often seen as an anomaly in the Austen canon. Austen criticism in recent decades has focused on this novel, highlighting the issues of gender, class, colonialism, religion, and education it amply and ambivalently presents.

As **Volume I** begins, Sir Thomas and Lady Bertram adopt their nine-year-old niece, Fanny Price. They are encouraged by the phony philanthropic spirit of Mrs. Norris, Lady Bertram's sister, who does not offer any material assistance herself. Fanny, the child of lower-middle-class relations, comes to live at stately Mansfield Park, where she is raised with Sir Thomas's daughters, though the class difference between them is strictly upheld. Scorned by her cousins, Fanny is "afraid of every body, ashamed of herself . . . and could scarcely speak to be heard, or without crying." Her cousins, Maria and Julia, doted on by their aunt, become the vain and confident "belles of the neighborhood."

The young Fanny is befriended by her sixteen-year-old cousin Edmund, who becomes her confidante. As they get older, she becomes his as well. She grows more comfortable at Mansfield Park, learning quickly and proving to have a calm, quiet temperament, but she is made to feel second-class and herself believes, "I can never be important to anyone." Edmund, as the second son, has difficulties of his own. Sir Thomas must sell the living on his estate, intended for Edmund when he is ordained a minister, to cover the debts incurred by his extravagant older son, Tom.

The main action of the story begins when Fanny is in her late teens. Sir Thomas departs for Antigua, where he has a sugar plantation. In the meantime, a circle of sociable young people gathers in the neighborhood around Mansfield Park. Maria becomes engaged to the fabulously wealthy but stupid Mr. Rushworth, and the young and beautiful Mary Crawford comes to live at the Mansfield parsonage with her half-sister, Mrs. Grant, bringing her charming brother Henry with her. Fanny, not considered equal to the young Bertrams, remains on the fringes of their activities. She is taken advantage of by everyone—benignly by the indolent Lady Bertram, who "cannot do without her," and more nastily by the miserly Mrs. Norris, who believes that Fanny owes her a perpetual debt of gratitude.

Fanny adores her cousin Edmund and finds herself "struggling against discontent and envy" when he reveals his admiration for Mary Crawford. Fanny and Edmund discuss Mary's dubious character, but he is nevertheless smitten. He borrows Fanny's horse to teach Mary to ride, and Fanny feels she is losing more than her favorite form of exercise. Edmund does not forget her, however, and intercedes on Fanny's behalf so that she can attend an outing to Rushworth's estate, Sotherton Court. This excursion provides important glimpses of the dynamics between the principal characters. Julia is eager to get Henry Crawford's attention, but Maria, already annoyed with Rushworth, is flirting dangerously with Crawford herself. Mary and Edmund leave Fanny alone to have their own tête-à-tête.

The outing establishes some of Austen's dominant themes. While touring the chapel of this ancient estate, Mary ridicules clergymen, to Edmund's consternation and regret. Debate ensues among them, with the right-minded Fanny stressing morality and tradition. Debate also centers upon the idea of "improvements" to the estate's grounds, reflecting popular trends in landscaping, larger concerns about the changing role of the gentry, and emergent "romanticism." Fanny and Edmund are portrayed as the only ones who truly appreciate nature for its moral worth. Fanny believes there would be less sorrow and wickedness in the world "if the sublimity of Nature were more attended to, and people were carried more out of themselves by contemplating such a scene."

Tom Bertram's friend John Yates arrives and encourages the group to stage a play. Edmund and Fanny strenuously object to such a plan with Sir Thomas away, but the enthusiasm of the others cannot be quelled. The play they choose, *Lover's Vows,* is particularly inappropriate, involving the story of one woman who has an illegitimate child and another who asks her tutor to marry her. Edmund is eventually persuaded to participate and is not terribly sorry to be playing opposite Mary as her lover. Crawford and Maria are also cast as lovers, Julia is excluded, and the dutiful

Fanny learns everyone's lines in the course of helping the slow-witted Rushworth.

The fun comes to an abrupt halt when Sir Thomas returns unexpectedly, making "a striking change in the ways of the family. . . . [Soon] it was all sameness and gloom." As **Volume II** begins, Maria, infatuated with Crawford, is disappointed when he leaves Mansfield for Bath. Pressured by her father and desiring wealth and status, she marries Mr. Rushworth anyway and departs for Brighton and London, with Julia for company. Meanwhile, Mary Crawford dreads Edmund's ordination, lamenting that he was "fixing himself in a situation which he must know she would never stoop to." She tries to persuade him to take up a more worldly occupation. He values honesty and tradition; she values riches. Nonetheless, he continues to desire her. Fanny, although she steels herself against disappointment, dreads the possibility of his marrying her.

With her cousins away, Fanny finds her "value increase" and is allowed to participate more in society. She begins to "bloom," acquiring greater personal grace and beauty. The bored Mary Crawford eagerly befriends her, and Henry Crawford returns to find her suddenly more attractive. He decides, deviously, to "conquer" her as he has so many other women, telling his sister that he intends to make "a small hole in Fanny Price's heart." Fanny is astonished and confused by his attention, but has no interest and is "grave, even reproachful" toward him, knowing of his unscrupulous behavior toward the affianced Maria Bertram.

Sir Thomas feels more and more proud of Fanny, admiring her goodness, and welcomes a visit from her beloved brother, William, a sailor. He also arranges a ball in her honor, where she shines. Crawford, unaccustomed to resistance, finds himself inadvertently falling in love and resolves to marry her. In an effort to overcome her indifference, he secures a promotion for William; though Fanny is extremely grateful and overjoyed, she rebukes Crawford's romantic attention.

Volume III opens with Crawford's formal proposal to Fanny via Sir Thomas. When Fanny admits that she has refused him, Sir Thomas is outraged. He cannot believe that she could turn down a match that so exceeds his expectations for her. Terribly upset by his anger, she still holds her ground. Edmund, though he does not advocate marrying without love, agrees with his father and tries to persuade Fanny to keep an open mind. Sir Thomas believes that time and patience will do the trick, and strategizes that a visit to the Prices, the family Fanny has not seen since she was a child, would "teach her the value of a good income."

Fanny is relieved to be given some space and travels to Portsmouth. She is distressed to find that she can scarcely endure the noisy, mismanaged household. Class issues are foregrounded. Austen attributes Fanny's class mobility not to her upbringing in a privileged environment, which would suggest that anyone would benefit from a similar transplantation, regardless of birth, but to an innate "natural delicacy." Crawford visits her in Portsmouth, and Sir Thomas's strategy seems to be working. As Austen wryly explains, "there is scarcely a young lady in the united kingdoms, who would not rather put up with the misfortune of being sought by a clever, agreeable man, than have him driven away by the vulgarity of her nearest relations." Fanny's heart remains elsewhere, however, and she dreads news from Edmund, who has resolved to propose marriage to Mary Crawford.

The news she receives is bad for Edmund and Fanny both. Mary is under the sway of her shrewd and materialistic city friends, and Edmund despairs of having any chance with her, lamenting, to Fanny's dismay, that he still "cannot give her up. . . . She is the only woman in the world whom I could ever think of as a wife." More bad news follows: Tom Bertram has fallen seriously ill, and there is concern that he has consumption. In a letter to Fanny, Mary admits that upon hearing that "poor Mr. Bertram has a bad chance of ultimate recovery," she began to think of his younger brother with greater interest—Edmund would inherit Mansfield Park in the event of Tom's death. Fanny is disgusted by Mary's greed. Soon thereafter, a still greater scandal breaks: Maria Rushworth has left her husband and eloped with Henry Crawford, a "matrimonial fracas" that is publicly advertised. Another blow falls on the Bertrams when Julia elopes with Yates.

Fanny returns to Mansfield. She is not sorry that Crawford has abandoned his pursuit of her, but Edmund is distraught that he has lost Mary forever: she has finally horrified him sufficiently by being insensitive to the immorality of what her brother and Maria have done. The scandal allows the good characters to be rewarded and the bad ones to be punished. Maria, divorced by Rushworth, wants to marry Crawford, but he is despondent that he has ruined his chances with Fanny, and they torture each other into hatred and finally separate. Maria is sent away to live in "another country" with the insufferable Mrs. Norris. Julia is forgiven by her father for her lesser sin. After a period of time that the narrator leaves the reader "at liberty to fix," Edmund transfers his affections to Fanny. With "true merit and true love, and no want of fortune or friends," they are married and live happily in the parsonage. ❈

List of Characters in
Mansfield Park

When **Fanny Price** arrives at Mansfield Park as a nine-year-old child, adopted by her wealthy aunt and uncle, she is painfully shy, full of self doubt and embarrassment, and prone to bursting into tears. As Edmund describes her, she has "an affectionate heart, and a strong desire of doing right; and he could perceive her to be farther entitled to attention, by great sensibility of her situation, and great timidity." As she grows up, she acquires patience and strong principles, becoming a model of modesty, piety, and duty. Unlike her vain and superficial cousins, Maria and Julia, Fanny is sensible and thoughtful of others. When Sir Thomas returns and finds the household disrupted, Edmund explains that "Fanny is the only one who has judged rightly throughout, who has been consistent." She grows into an attractive woman, and Henry Crawford falls in love with her for her "ineffable sweetness and patience" and "unpretending gentleness." She, however, does not return his love, and waits for the object of her affections, Edmund Bertram.

Kind and high-principled, **Edmund Bertram** "was not pleasant by any common rule, he talked no nonsense, he paid no compliments, his opinions were unbending, his attentions tranquil and simple. There was a charm, perhaps, in his sincerity, his steadiness, his integrity." The second son of a distinguished wealthy family, he plans to be a clergyman, but his financial security is threatened when the living that is promised to him is leased to pay his older brother's debts. He is Fanny Price's friend and champion from childhood, ensuring that she is not completely neglected by his otherwise selfish family. He falls in love with the unworthy Mary Crawford, but at the end of the novel realizes that Fanny is a better choice for a wife.

Mary Crawford is worldly, wealthy, and "remarkably pretty." Her charm and "lively dark eye" make her irresistible to Edmund Bertram. She turns out to be selfish and vain, motivated primarily by her ambition for status and wealth. She resembles Elizabeth Bennet (*Pride and Prejudice*) in many ways, but the moral attitude toward a headstrong, sexually attractive woman is strongly negative in this novel. Critics have considered this change: "Did [Austen] suffer some inner compulsion to revenge herself upon her own imagination, to scourge her wit, to punish the saucy Elizabeth Bennet by recasting her as that shallow, worldling-siren, Mary Crawford?" Claudia Johnson asks in her introduction to *Mansfield Park*.

Henry Crawford is, as his sister puts it, "the most horrible flirt that can be imagined." He is "not handsome," but is wealthy and stylish and has such an engaging demeanor that he is quickly the favorite of young women, wooing them with "the usual attack of gallantry and compliment." The one woman who touches his heart is Fanny Price, but she is unimpressed, and he eventually gives in to frivolous temptation and commits adultery with Maria Bertram Rushworth. The final judgment upon him is that he was "ruined by early independence and bad domestic example."

Sir Thomas Bertram is a strict and respectable Baronet and Member of Parliament who exemplifies paternal authority. He has business with a sugar plantation in Antigua that calls him away from England for a large portion of the novel. As Mrs. Grant explains, "He has a fine dignified manner, which suits the head of such a house, and keeps every body in their place. Lady Bertram seems more of a cipher now than when he is at home; and nobody else can keep Mrs. Norris in order." He is domineering and inspires fear, but is capable of fairness and seeing the error of his ways.

Lady Bertram is "a woman who spent her days in sitting nicely dressed on a sofa, doing some long piece of needle-work, of little use and no beauty, thinking more of her pug than her children, but very indulgent to the latter, when it did not put herself to inconvenience." Nonetheless, she comes to appreciate Fanny genuinely by the end of the novel, and proves to have a warmer regard for her husband than most had imagined. ❁

Critical Views on
Mansfield Park

WARREN ROBERTS ON RELIGION AND FRANCOPHOBIA

[Warren Roberts is professor of history at the State University of New York at Albany. In this excerpt Roberts explains that English panic about the French Revolution, with its secular ideology, was often linked to fears about the waning influence of religion. When Mary Crawford ridicules religion, and Fanny and Edmund defend it, Austen suggests the importance upholding English traditions and defending against the "Frenchified" culture Mary represents.]

In contrast to Mary Crawford's "French" levity and irreverence was Fanny's "English" sobriety and serious conception of religion and its impact on family life. To her it was unfortunate that the Rushworths had abandoned family worship, which she considered a custom that should not have been discontinued. "It was a valuable part of the former times. There is something in a chapel and chaplain so much in character with a great house, with one's idea of what such a household should be! A whole family assembling regularly for the purpose of prayer, is fine!" While the spiritual importance of worship was not dwelled upon, the danger of irreverence was, indicating Austen's objection to the modern, fashionable tendency to be religiously indifferent, if not to ridicule religion. For Austen and many of her contemporaries religion was important as a force of social continuity and a safeguard against the secular and atheistic ideology of the French Revolution. Mary Crawford was not atheistic, but she was secular and did ridicule religion. So the discussion is about family worship, it is about religion as a force of family and social cohesion, it is about the dangers of the modern and fashionable mockery of religion, and it establishes a dichotomy between rival outlooks and systems of value. The dialogue shows Edmund and Fanny as the upholders of tradition and custom, and Mary Crawford represents attitudes that are alien and incompatible with settled English country ways.

After leaving the chapel, Mary asked Edmund why he wanted to become a clergyman, saying that he could not distinguish himself in such a profession. Edmund acknowledged that a clergyman could not be "high in state or fashion", and "must not head mobs, or set the ton in dress", but explained that he was the guardian of "religion and morals, and consequently of the manners which result from their influence". Mary wondered if two sermons a week were adequate to "govern the conduct and fashion the manners of a large congregation for the rest of the week? One scarcely sees a clergyman out of his pulpit." This remark led to a discussion of religious life in London and the country, Edmund contending that the clergy's greatest influence was not in great cities but local parishes, and that morality depended largely on the extent of that influence. The manners that drew their substance from morality did not consist of good breeding, refinement and courtesy, but right conduct and principles. This was the calling that Edmund hoped to answer. While the obvious contrast in this passage is between morality and manners in London and the country, the English-French dichotomy in the previous dialogue is also present here. Upon reaffirming his decision to enter the clergy Edmund explained that there was not the least wit in his nature, and that "I am a very matter of fact, plain spoken being, and may blunder on the borders of a repartee for half a hour together without striking it out." In this passage Austen had in mind a distinctively English type, one who was not polished, refined, clever, urbane, and cosmopolitan, but serious, introspective, stolid, direct and forthright; the former, refined type was French or—to be more exact—bore the stamp of French culture.

—Warren Roberts, *Jane Austen and the French Revolution* (New York: St. Martin's Press, 1979): pp. 34–35.

MARY POOVEY ON DISCIPLINE AND REFORM

[Mary Poovey, professor of English at New York University, is the author of *Uneven Developments: The Ideological Work of Gender in Mid-Victorian England*, and *Making a Social Body: British Cultural Formation, 1830–1864*. In this extract Poovey suggests that Austen, in her later novels, saw women's discipline as a way of reforming the contradictions of her society from within, creating Fanny Price to emphasize how "principled" female behavior could guard against the hazards of "anarchic desire."]

That Jane Austen did have a sense of her role as a professional author, writing primarily for an intelligent audience, becomes an important factor in our understanding of her last novels. Though she was obviously enamored of the wit, the charm, and the relative popularity of *Pride and Prejudice*, she now desired to turn to "a complete change of subject" (*JAL*, 2:298; 29 January 1813), and that fact, and the particular subject she chose, suggest that she was now beginning to sense that irony, and the moral ambiguity it often entailed, would blur her more serious didactic design. Perhaps because her own personal experience was showing her both the perils of the female situation and the inadequacy of escaping into the purely aesthetic consolation of romance, she wanted to use her art to confront some of the problems that made romantic escape attractive. In order to do so, Austen withheld from her readers both the "playfulness and epigrammatism" of *Pride and Prejudice* (*JAL*, 2:300; 4 February 1813) and the immediate gratification provided by a heroine with whom it was flattering—and rewarding—to identify. Austen was aware that doing so might cost her what popularity she had acquired. She acknowledged, for example, that *Mansfield Park* was "not half so entertaining" as her last novel (*JAL*, 2:317; 3 July 1813), and she predicted that those who appreciated *Pride and Prejudice* would find *Emma* "inferior in wit" (*JAL*, 2:443; 11 December 1815). But Austen was beginning to see that challenging her readers' expectations and desires was a necessary first step toward reforming the social practices that currently helped to frustrate female self-expression and fulfillment. By educating her readers to the dangers of uninhibited desires, Austen might be able to convince them that the controls exercised by the institutions of patriarchal society were necessary. By then suggesting that principled feeling could, in turn, reform these social institutions, she could argue that discipline was not only necessary but desirable. Particularly through dramatizing such "principled" yet passionate heroines as Fanny Price and Anne Elliot, Austen would be able to show how bourgeois ideology could be purged of its contradictions and how, when it was so reformed, it could accommodate female feeling without driving a woman's energy into self-destructive or anarchic forms. ⟨. . .⟩

Beside the charming, outspoken Elizabeth Bennet, Fanny Price holds little appeal for many readers, but as a response to the complex dangers threatening the values of traditional society, she promises a more convincing solution than Elizabeth Bennet could offer. For though Elizabeth's impertinence could be schooled into love, the individualistic energy she represented was ominously akin to one of the primary antagonists of social order. By contrast, Fanny Price is outwardly everything a textbook Proper Lady should be; she is dependent, self-effacing, and apparently free of impermissible desires. If so ideal an exemplar of femininity could be made both sympathetic and powerful, Austen would be able to demonstrate how traditional society could be regenerated from within its own values and institutions.

—Mary Poovey, *The Proper Lady and the Woman Writer* (Chicago: University of Chicago Press, 1984): pp. 211–212.

BREAN HAMMOND ON SOCIAL MOBILITY

[Brean S. Hammond is professor of English at the University College of Wales at Aberystwyth and the author of books on Alexander Pope, Jonathan Swift, and politics and satire in the eighteenth century. Drawing on the Marxist theories of Fredric Jameson, in which a literary work can be reconfigured as a "dialogue between antagonistic class discourses," Hammond argues that Fanny Price's rise in class status requires the ideological "prevarication" of "natural aristocracy."]

Fanny's experience in Portsmouth ⟨. . .⟩ permits us to catch sight of the novel's ideological contradictions. What is the significance, to return to our earlier question, of Fanny's spectacular migration up the social scale? Such migrations occur in earlier novels—witness Fielding's *Tom Jones*—but in Fielding this is usually expressed through a romance motif in which the protagonist discovers his true gentility prior to getting the girl and the estate. *Mansfield Park*, by contrast, renders social mobility in the mystified notion of "natural aristocracy". The irresistible rise of Fanny Price does not configure the possibility of any general class mobility—the Price family as a whole is not Mansfield material—but Fanny's sister Susan is, in a similarly mystified way, marked out as suitable stock for transplanting to the more nourishing soil of Mansfield. (Susan, we are told, "had an innate taste for the genteel and well-appointed" and it distressed Fanny that she should be left in the parental home.) Yet Austen's protagonists are consciously constructed *against the grain* of novelistic treatments of female heroism ("No one who had ever seen Catherine Morland in her infancy would have supposed her born to be an heroine", is the opening sentence of *Northanger Abbey*) and it is clear that by comparison to earlier characters like Elizabeth Bennet and Emma Woodhouse, Fanny Price represents a new narrative challenge: a woman who is not spirited or precocious and who is rendered passive by her social inferiority and introversion, who nevertheless becomes a magnetic centre of attraction. In the end, however, no adequate explanation is brought to bear on Fanny's exceptional status and she remains a "heroine". We *might* read, there is a *danger* of us reading, this plot as an illustration of the aristocracy's need for patrilineal and matrilineal repair: a transfusion of bourgeois blood is needed to put the aristocracy back on its feet. I suggest, however, that the text resists this reading, offering us instead a Fanny Price who is "naturally" an aristocrat. Her marriage to Edmund comes to seem virtually endogamous. They are more like brother and sister than husband and wife, and Fanny can be taken into the family without creating the impression of any accommodation. The novel apparently dramatizes a process of the English landed aristocracy's putting its own house in order and thereby resisting external challenges; but it represses an alternative reading of its significance, which would endow the scions of the Price family with the more dynamic social energies. In other words, the logic of the plot, which enacts the social advancement of lower middle-class individuals, undermines the aristocratic-conservative interests that the fable is invented to defend; and the only way to avoid the reader drawing this conclusion is to prevaricate between a construction of the Prices as "typical" and a construction of them as "exceptional". Natural aristocracy, as applied to Fanny and Susan (less so to William because he, after all, has a social structure for advancement, a career ladder), is the ideally obfuscatory, perfectly ideological tool for accomplishing this work.

—Brean S. Hammond, "The Political Unconscious in *Mansfield Park*," in *Mansfield Park,* ed. Nigel Wood (Philadelphia: Open University Press, 1993): pp. 82–83.

[Edward Said, professor and Chair of Comparative Literature at Columbia University, is an important post-colonial
theorist and scholar whose books include *Orientalism, The
Politics of Dispossession,* and *Culture and Imperialism.* In
this controversial discussion of *Mansfield Park,* focusing on
Sir Thomas Bertram's business in Antigua, Said examines
the "sordid history" behind the Bertram's wealth, and the
"hidden or allusive" imperial context of Austen's novels.]

Take once again the casual references to Antigua, the ease with
which Sir Thomas's needs in England are met by a Caribbean
sojourn, the uninflected, unreflective citations of Antigua (or the
Mediterranean, or India, which is where Lady Bertram, in a fit of
distracted impatience, requires that William should go "'that I
may have a shawl. I think I will have two shawls.'") They stand for
a significance "out there" that frames the genuinely important
action *here,* but not for a great significance. Yet these signs of
"abroad" include, even as they repress, a rich and complex history,
which has since achieved a status that the Bertrams, the Prices, and
Austen herself would not, could not recognize. To call this "the
Third World" begins to deal with the realities but by no means
exhausts the political or cultural history.

We must first take stock of *Mansfield Park*'s prefigurations of a
later English history as registered in fiction. The Bertrams' usable
colony in *Mansfield Park* can be read as pointing forward to Charles
Gould's San Tomé mine in *Nostromo,* or to the Wilcoxes' Imperial
and West African Rubber Company in Forster's *Howards End,* or to
any of these distant but convenient treasure spots in *Great Expectations,* Jean Rhys's *Wide Sargasso Sea, Heart of Darkness*—resources
to be visited, talked about, described, or appreciated for domestic
reasons, for local metropolitan benefit. If we think ahead to these
other novels, Sir Thomas's Antigua readily acquires a slightly greater
density than the discrete, reticent appearances it makes in the
pages of *Mansfield Park.* And already our reading of the novel
begins to open up at those points where ironically Austen was
most economical and her critics most (dare one say it?) negligent.
Her "Antigua" is therefore not just a slight but a definite way of
marking the outer limits of what Williams calls domestic improvements, or a quick allusion to the mercantile venturesomeness of

acquiring overseas dominions as a source for local fortunes, or one reference among many attesting to a historical sensibility suffused not just with manners and courtesies but with contests of ideas, struggles with Napoleonic France, awareness of seismic economic and social change during a revolutionary period in world history.

Second, we must see "Antigua" held in a precise place in Austen's moral geography, and in her prose, by historical changes that her novel rides like a vessel on a mighty sea. The Bertrams could not have been possible without the slave trade, sugar, and the colonial planter class; as a social type Sir Thomas would have been familiar to eighteenth- and early-nineteenth-century readers who knew the powerful influence of the class through politics, plays (like Cumberland's *The West Indian*), and many other public activities (large houses, famous parties and social rituals, well-known commercial enterprises, celebrated marriages). As the old system of protected monopoly gradually disappeared and as a new class of settler-planters displaced the old absentee system, the West Indian interest lost dominance: cotton manufacture, an even more open system of trade, and abolition of the slave trade reduced the power and prestige of people like the Bertrams, whose frequency of sojourn in the Caribbean then decreased. ⟨. . .⟩

The question of interpretation, indeed of writing itself, is tied to the question of interests, which we have seen are at work in aesthetic as well as historical writing, then and now. We must not say that since *Mansfield Park* is a novel, its affiliations with a sordid history are irrelevant or transcended, not only because it is irresponsible to do so, but because we know too much to say so in good faith. Having read *Mansfield Park* as part of the structure of an expanding imperialist venture, one cannot simply restore it to the canon of "great literary masterpieces"—to which it most certainly belongs—and leave it at that. Rather, I think, the novel steadily, if unobtrusively, opens up a broad expanse of domestic imperialist culture without which Britain's subsequent acquisition of territory would not have been possible.

—Edward Said, *Culture and Imperialism* (New York: Alfred A. Knopf, 1993): pp. 93–95.

BRIAN SOUTHAM ON THE SLAVE TRADE

[An important scholar of Jane Austen, T. S. Eliot, and Tennyson, Brian Southam has taught at Oxford and universities in London. He is the editor of *Jane Austen: The Critical Heritage* and co-editor of *The Jane Austen Handbook*. In this essay, Southam analyzes evidence in the novel and dates Sir Thomas's return from Antigua as October 1812, five years after the abolition of the slave trade in 1807. The details of the historical situation surrounding Sir Thomas's involvement with a colonial plantation shed light on Fanny's question about the slave trade in Chapter 21.]

With the advent of the slave and colonialist perspectives, the dating of the story becomes important to our understanding of *Mansfield Park*, since the Bertrams are financed by the income from their Antigua estate and Sir Thomas takes his journey there in an attempt to halt its decline—successfully, as it turns out. Although these circumstances play a significant part in the first half of the story and resonate throughout the novel, traditional accounts of *Mansfield Park* have ignored the purpose of Sir Thomas's voyage (some describe it, using Austen's own word, as merely a visit on "business") and have treated the journey as no more than a device to get the head of the family out of the way and allow the young people to run wild. But to accept the historical force of Austen's portrait is to view Sir Thomas not just as a patriarchal English country gentleman but also in his "colonial" role as an absentee plantation owner, in Parliament an active member of the West Indian lobby, now compelled by "some recent losses on his West Indian Estate" to return to Antigua and (as we may suppose) take over the running of the plantation from the resident manager and restore it to prosperity. "Fat managers and lean employees" was the uncomfortable adage current on the island.

A variety of datings has been proposed for the action of the novel, some of which open up wholly misleading lines of interpretation: 1803–6 or 1805–7 sets Sir Thomas's visit just ahead of the abolition of the slave trade in 1807; whereas 1808–9 or 1808–10 give us post-abolitionist readings. Equally, in Chapter Twenty-One, Fanny's "slave trade" question to Sir Thomas carried a very different significance in 1812 than it would if asked in earlier years. It was a question which Fanny wanted to follow up with others. But she was deterred from doing so by the "dead silence" that followed, her cousins "sitting by without speaking a word, or seeming at all interested in the subject." We are left to wonder about Sir Thomas's reply. Charitably, we can suppose that he answers Fanny fully and to her satisfaction. But Jane Austen glides over the point, leaving it wholly unresolved, perhaps even weighing the balance against him. A moment earlier, Fanny has been telling Edmund how she loves to hear Sir Thomas talking of the West Indies, how she "could listen to him for an hour together. It entertains *me* more than many other things have done." Earlier, Sir Thomas was "communicative and chatty . . . as to his voyage." Now, the "dead silence" hints that his loquacity may have dried up at the mention of slaves. As if to underline the point, Austen later restores Sir Thomas's animation when he comes to talk to William Price about "the balls of Antigua", a recreation that the young midshipman may also have enjoyed on his West Indies tour of duty.

The precise interpretation of this scene—of Fanny's questions, asked and unasked, of the "dead silence", of the cousins' "seeming" absence of interest—turns crucially on the issue of dating. Some critics fasten immediately on Fanny's reference to the slave trade and conclude, over-hastily, that her question to Sir Thomas must have been put before the Abolition Act became law in March 1807. But this is to misunderstand the historical situation. The Act came into force in two stages: from May 1, 1807, no ship with slaves on board was permitted to sail from any port in the British Empire unless legally cleared before that date: and from March 1, 1808, no slaves were to be landed. By the letter of the Act, for Britain and its overseas possessions, the slave trade was ended: "hereby utterly abolished, prohibited, and declared to be unlawful". Declaration, of course, is one thing, enforcement another. This branch of commerce, recognized, sanctioned and encouraged for 250 years, now went underground.

—Brian Southam, "The Silence of the Bertrams," *Times Literary Supplement* (February 17, 1995). Reprinted in *Mansfield Park*, ed. Claudia Johnson (New York: W. W. Norton, 1998): pp. 494–495.

CLAUDIA JOHNSON ON MONEY

[Claudia Johnson is professor of English at Princeton University and the author of *Equivocal Beings: Politics, Gender, and Sentimentality in the 1790s* and *Jane Austen: Women, Politics, and the Novel*. In this extract from her introduction to the Norton Critical Edition of *Mansfield Park*, which she edited, Johnson provides an informative discussion of the annual incomes of Austen's characters: How rich *is* Rushworth?]

Few subjects fascinate students reading Austen for the first time more than money, and for good reason: Austen's characters themselves are both extremely interested in their neighbors' annual incomes and extremely well-informed about them. Their houses, grounds, and gardens, their trips to London, their carriages, their servants, their governesses, their pianos, and the fruit on their tables are signs of wealth and status.

During Austen's time, one's wealth is typically described as a yearly disposable income, a figure in turn calculated by multiplying the principal of one's inheritance by 5 percent (the interest earned by investing in 5 percent government funds). But determining the actual value of money during Austen's time is a greater challenge. In recent years, those of us accustomed to currency based on dollars rather than pounds sterling have been advised to multiply each pound sterling by anywhere from 33, 60, or 200 times in order to determine dollar equivalencies for the United States in the late twentieth century, formulas that would put Mr. Rushworth's yearly disposable income of $12,000 at around $396,000, $720,000 or $2,900,000 a year. Of course, scholars and economists are also quick to add that such formulas are misleading. First, the economy during Austen's time was still principally landed and agrarian, which means among many other things that the basic cost of consumer items is not comparable to their cost today, in an urban and industrial economy. Cloth, for example, which was not mass manufactured, was very expensive, and food generally cheaper. Second, wealth itself was distributed among a much smaller number of people than is the case today. When G. E. Mingay says that only four hundred families among the landed gentry during Austen's time had annual incomes within the range of £5,000 and £50,000, with the average among these at £10,000 (Darcy's annual income in *Pride and Prejudice*), we get some idea of the fabulousness of Rushworth's £12,000 a year in *Mansfield Park*, and some insight into Sir Thomas's motives for wanting his daughter Maria to proceed with her marriage to Rushworth, even though he knows she does not love him.

If the stupendous wealth of Rushworth is the upper limit in Austen's novels, at the lower end is what her characters call a "competence," which Edward Copeland had aptly defined as "the bottom line of gentility, increasing and decreasing with the pretensions of its possessor to rank and status." In *Mansfield Park*, Edmund's living at Thornton Lacey is £700 a year, and this figure, twice as much as what was minimally necessary for a bachelor, is the bottom range of a competence for a married couple. At the end of *Sense and Sensibility*, the sensible Elinor Dashwood attains her dream of a competence when she and Edward Ferrars marry on a combined annual income of £850. Mr. and Mrs. Norris had an income of about £1,000, which makes Mrs. Norris's stinginess more irrational. Commanding an extremely ample fortune of £4,000 a year himself, Henry Crawford calls Edmund's income "a fine thing for a younger brother" partly because he assumes that Edmund will reside at Mansfield Park and that his living will be pocket money. The worldly Mary Crawford, with a taste for London life, is alarmed by Edmund's unambitious contentment with a competence. Five percent interest on her fortune of £20,000 would bring in £1,000 a year, and this money was more than a competence; indeed, it was sufficient even to cover some of the elegancies of genteel life, such as a carriage. Twice that much would be considered wealth for the minor gentry. More opulent luxuries such as a house in London required a yearly income of £5,000 or more.

—Claudia Johnson, "A Note on Money in Austen's Novels." In *Mansfield Park*, ed. Claudia Johnson (New York: W. W. Norton, 1998): pp. xiii–xiv.

Plot Summary of
Emma

The last novel published in Austen's lifetime, *Emma* is often considered her most perfectly constructed book. It focuses on the aspirations and foibles of 21-year-old Emma Woodhouse, the highest ranking woman in Highbury, a picturesque English town. Emma runs her father's household and her social circle with elegance and spirit, but entangles herself and others in the folly of her imaginative illusions. Austen observes her heroine from a skillful distance, enabling the reader to be aware of her flaws and still find her endearing.

As the novel opens, Emma is lonely without her governess and friend, Miss Taylor, who has just married her neighbor, Mr. Weston. She is left with the company of her eccentric father and Mr. Knightley, the owner of Donwell Abbey and a close family friend. Mr. Knightley, who is sixteen years older than Emma and has watched her grow up, has the clearest perspective on her. She is a self-important busybody, but Mr. Knightley and Mrs. Weston agree that despite her faults, she is "an excellent creature." Mr. Knightley foresees changes: "I should like to see Emma in love, and in some doubt of a return." She herself, however, declares that she will never marry.

Emma takes an interest in the naïve and beautiful Harriet Smith, a parlour boarder at a local school. Merely "the natural daughter of somebody," the seventeen-year-old Harriet lacks breeding and rank, and Emma takes her under her wing: "*She* would notice her; she would improve her; she would detach her from her bad acquaintances, and introduce her into good society." Emma imagines that she can arrange a match between Harriet and Mr. Elton, the vicar. In the meantime, Robert Martin, an honest farmer Harriet has liked for some time, proposes to her. Insisting that Harriet is destined for better things, Emma counsels her to refuse him. Mr. Knightley, who knows and admires Martin, criticizes Emma for her interference.

Emma soon learns the error of her ways. One snowy night, Mr. Elton manages to get Emma alone and declares his love for her. She is mortified to discover that he has had no interest in Harriet at all, and instead was courting *her*. Austen makes her snobbish astonishment clear, as the narrator slips into Emma's voice: Mr. Elton must have known that "the Woodhouses had been settled for several generations at Hartfield, the younger branch of a very ancient family, and that the Eltons were nobody." Harriet, who has become infatuated with Mr. Elton, is heartbroken. Emma is chastened and resolves "to do such things no more."

Emma is anxious to maintain her position as first lady of Highbury. She interacts with townspeople and cottagers as chief consumer, dispenser of charity, and standard of elegance. When she pays her obligatory visits to Miss Bates, a loquacious spinster, she is forced to encounter her least favorite person, Jane Fairfax. Cool and accomplished, Jane shows up Emma at the piano and annoys her with her "odious" composure. Another woman also challenges Emma's superiority, albeit ineffectually. The resilient Mr. Elton soon finds another wealthy woman to marry and brings his insufferable wife to Highbury, where she is a continual affront to Emma with her "air of pert pretension and underbred finery."

After much anticipation and delay, Frank Churchill, Mr. Weston's son from his first marriage, arrives in Highbury. Raised by wealthy relatives (and taking their name), Frank is handsome, well-connected, and, in Emma's eyes, worthy of her—her highest possible compliment. He is attentive and flattering, and the Westons encourage a match between them. He is secretly engaged, however, to Jane Fairfax. In light of this information, which we learn late in the novel, many of Emma's and Frank's exchanges are wonderfully ironic, as Emma blunders unwittingly into half-truths.

Emma tends to draw the wrong conclusions from her observations. When Jane is mysteriously given a piano, for example, Emma suspects that she is secretly in love with Mr. Dixon, her adoptive sister's husband. Frank Churchill is soon called away by his demanding aunt, Mrs. Churchill, and Emma is disappointed, beginning to believe that she is in love with him. When the departing Frank appears to be on the verge of proposing to her, however, she quickly changes the subject. She remains ambivalent about marriage and about her feelings for Frank. (In truth, he was about to tell her about his engagement to Jane.) When Frank returns, Emma discovers that her feelings for him have waned and observes that he also appears "less in love."

Harriet recovers from her heartbreak over Mr. Elton. At a much-anticipated ball, she is snubbed by him, but pleased when Mr. Knightley dances with her. Soon thereafter, she is assailed by a pack of gypsies on the road and rescued by Frank Churchill. Emma is sure that the event will induce Harriet and Frank to fall in love, and she schemes for this new match for Harriet. When Harriet tells her that she is in love with someone who is greatly her superior, Emma believes that Harriet's object is Frank, and approves. She misunderstands Harriet's explanation: the man in question has "rendered her a service." Emma thinks Harriet refers to Frank, who saved her from the gypsies, but she means *Mr. Knightley*, who rescued her at the dance.

Two summer outings heighten tensions. While strawberry picking at Donwell Abbey, Emma observes Harriet and Mr. Knightley in private conversation and sees Jane Fairfax leaving in unhappy agitation. Soon thereafter, the group goes to Box Hill, where a feeling of uneasiness pervades the company. Frank and Emma flirt shamelessly, and Emma insults the good-hearted Miss Bates with a caustic remark. Mr. Knightley sternly reprimands her, and she is deeply upset by his disapproval, resolving to be more worthy of his regard.

Several events occur in rapid succession to unravel mysteries. Mrs. Churchill dies suddenly, and Frank rushes to Highbury just in time to reconcile with his beloved Jane and keep her from going into service as a governess. Their engagement is made public, and it is revealed that his flirtation with Emma was "a blind to conceal his real situation with another." Everyone is shocked. The Westons are worried that Emma will be crushed, but she assures them that she does not love Frank. Frank explains himself, describes the obstacles and recent misunderstandings in his relationship with Jane, and apologizes for his selfish disregard for others in "playing a most dangerous game."

Emma is worried about Harriet, "extremely angry with herself" for encouraging the girl in *another* ill-fated attachment. She is mortified to discover that Harriet never cared for Frank Churchill at all. She loves Mr. Knightley, and he appears to return her feelings. Emma is indignant and unaccountably upset. She has a sudden self-revelation: "It darted through her with the speed of an arrow that Mr. Knightley must marry no one but herself! Her own conduct, as well as her own heart, was before her in the same few minutes." She realizes her own blindness and true motivations with regret and shame. "With insufferable vanity had she believed herself in the secret of everybody's feelings; with unpardonable arrogance proposed to arrange everybody's destiny." She believes she has paid for her mistakes by losing Mr. Knightley, the person most dear to her.

Mr. Knightley and Emma at last have a conversation that is the novel's climactic scene. Like the Westons, he is concerned that Emma is heartbroken about Frank, but she assures him that she is not. He is greatly relieved and about to confess deep feelings, but Emma suspects he is going to tell her about his love for Harriet, and silences him. He interprets her rebuke as a rejection and despairs. Emma, however, believes she must steel herself against losing him to Harriet, and reopens the conversation. When he proclaims his love for *her*, she is overcome with happiness. He has no thoughts of Harriet. To him, Emma has always been the "sweetest and best of all creatures, faultless in spite of all her faults." They become engaged.

Austen emphasizes that conflicts are resolved and harmony restored only when the characters know their own true feelings as well as their appropriate social positions. One final problem stands in the way of Emma's complete happiness—her regret about Harriet. This situation is resolved and past wrongs are redressed when Emma stops interfering. Robert Martin resumes his courtship of Harriet, and this time she is free to follow her own heart, accepting him happily. When this third couple is reconciled, the situation is "all right, all open, all equal." ❀

List of Characters in
Emma

Emma Woodhouse is "handsome, clever, and rich," a young woman of fortune and rank with great personal charm. Loved and admired by those around her, she has grown up self-centered and self-important: "The real evils, indeed, of Emma's situation were the power of having rather too much her own way, and a disposition to think a little too well of herself." As Mr. Knightley explains,

> Emma is spoiled by being the cleverest of her family. At ten years old she had the misfortune of being able to answer questions which puzzled her sister at seventeen. She was always quick and assured; Isabella slow and diffident. And ever since she was twelve, Emma has been mistress of the house and of you all. In her mother she lost the only person able to cope with her.

Well-intentioned, but often deluded as to her own motives or blinded by her imagination, she is prone to matchmaking and meddling. Austen herself declared her to be a character "no one but myself will much like," but Emma's warmth, enthusiasm, and capacity for change make her one of Austen's most likeable creations.

George Knightley, "a sensible man about seven or eight-and-thirty, was not only a very old and intimate friend of the family, but particularly connected with it, as the elder brother of [Emma's sister] Isabella's husband." With his noble principles and "tall, firm, upright figure," he epitomizes a "gentlemanlike manner" and "natural grace." He displays "that upright integrity, that strict adherence to truth and principle, that disdain of trick and littleness" that Emma believes the perfect man should have. He has the clearest understanding of all the characters. Intelligent and insightful, he is capable of interpreting "symptoms," most often correctly. His love for Emma, however, gives him some uncertainty: he is hurt by her apparent attachment to Frank and overjoyed to learn, finally, that she returns his love.

Frank Churchill is "a *very* good-looking young man" [Austen's italics]. With his "well-bred ease of manner, and a readiness to talk," he quickly wins over Emma, but his behavior is suspicious. In Mr. Knightley's jealous opinion, Frank is "proud, luxurious, and selfish," able to "adapt his conversation to the taste of everybody, and [having] the power as well as the wish of being universally agreeable." He turns out to have been deceiving everyone, but forgivably, since he acted out of love for Jane.

Jane Fairfax, Miss Bates's orphan niece, is "very elegant, remarkably elegant" with her deep grey eyes. Raised by the well-to-do Colonel Campbell, her late father's friend, she grows up with the advantages of his own daughter. Though Jane is exceptionally accomplished, her "situation" requires that she be sent out to work as a governess in the near future. Her musical talent and implacable calm make her an object of Emma's jealousy. In Emma's view, Jane is "wrapped up in a cloak of politeness . . . determined to hazard nothing. She was disgustingly, suspiciously reserved." When Jane reveals that she has suffered great anxiety and jealousy herself in the course of her secret engagement, she appears more human.

Mr. Woodhouse, Emma's father, is coddled by his adoring daughters, especially Emma, who treats his "peculiarities and fidgetiness" with indulgence and loyalty. His reluctance to go out, abhorrence of change, and lamentations over the tragic fates of women who succumb to matrimony make for wonderful comic moments in the novel. He is adamant about the evils of wedding-cake, for example, and urges others not to eat it, since "he could never believe other people to be different from himself."

Miss Bates, with Mr. Woodhouse, contributes much to the novel's comedy. A middle-aged unmarried woman, she lives with her elderly mother on a very small income. She is an "eternal talker," full of "anxious inquiries" and "cheerful communications," but she is beyond reproach because of her "universal good-will." Emma has little patience for her, finding her "so silly, so satisfied, so smiling, so prosing, so undistinguishing and unfastidious, and so apt to tell everything relative to everybody. She dotes on her beloved niece, Jane Fairfax.

Harriet Smith is beautiful, but naïve. Emma Woodhouse decides to take a hand in finding a match for Harriet, with disastrous results. In the end, Emma resolves to stop meddling and Harriet marries the man she truly loves, Robert Martin. ❀

Critical Views on
Emma

[Sir Walter Scott (1771–1832), Scottish novelist and poet, is best known for his ballads and historical novels. His most famous works include the poems *The Lay of the Last Minstrel* and *The Lady of the Lake,* and the novels *Waverly* and *Ivanhoe.* In this early review, the first major critical notice that Austen received, Scott praises her mastery of characterization and fidelity to "common incidents," so unlike the idealized portraits and far-fetched occurrences of sentimental romances, as the achievement of "the modern novel."]

⟨A⟩ style of novel has arisen, within the last fifteen or twenty years, differing from the former in the points upon which the interest hinges; neither alarming our credulity nor amusing our imagination by wild variety of incident, or by those pictures of romantic affection and sensibility, which were formerly as certain attributes of fictitious characters as they are of rare occurrence among those who actually live and die. The substitute for these excitements, which had lost much of their poignancy by the repeated and injudicious use of them, was the art of copying from nature as she really exists in the common walks of life, and presenting to the reader, instead of the splendid scenes of an imaginary world, a correct and striking representation of that which is daily taking place around him.

In adventuring upon this task, the author makes obvious sacrifices, and encounters peculiar difficulty. He who paints from the *le beau idéal,* if his scenes and sentiments are striking and interesting, is in a great measure exempted from the difficult task of reconciling them with the ordinary probabilities of life: but he who paints a scene of common occurrence, places his composition within that extensive range of criticism which general experience offers to every reader. The resemblance of a statue of Hercules we must take on the artist's judgment; but every one can criticize that which is presented as the portrait of a friend, or neighbour. Something more than a mere sign-post likeness is also demanded. The portrait must have spirit and character, as well as resemblance; and being deprived of all that, according to Bayes, goes "to elevate and surprize," it must make amends by displaying depth of knowledge and dexterity of execution. We, therefore, bestow no mean compliment upon the author of *Emma*, when we say that, keeping close to common incidents, and to such characters as occupy the ordinary walks of life, she has produced sketches of such spirit and originality, that we never miss the excitation which depends upon a narrative of uncommon events, arising from the consideration of minds, manners, and sentiments, greatly above our own. In this class she stands almost alone; for the scenes of Miss Edgeworth are laid in higher life, varied by more romantic incident, and by her remarkable power of embodying and illustrating national character. But the author of *Emma* confines herself chiefly to the middling class of society; her most distinguished characters do not rise greatly above well-bred country gentlemen and ladies; and those which are sketched with most originality and precision, belong to a class rather below that standard. The narrative of all her novels is composed of such common occurrences as may have fallen under the observation of most folks; and her dramatis personæ conduct themselves upon the motives and principles which the readers may recognize as ruling their own and that of most of their acquaintances. The kind of moral, also, which these novels inculcate, applies equally to the paths of common life, as will best appear from a short notice of the author's former works, with a more full abstract of that which we at present have under consideration.

—Walter Scott, unsigned review of *Emma* in *Quarterly Review* (March 1816). Reprinted in *Jane Austen: The Critical Heritage, Vol. 1 (1811–1870)*, ed. B. C. Southam, (New York: Routledge, 1995): pp. 63–64.

[Marvin Mudrick is the author of critical books on Austen and Joseph Conrad and editor of two collections of critical essays. In this passage from Mudrick's pivotal 1952 study of Austen, which emerges from a New Critical emphasis on verbal and dramatic irony, he argues that Austen's portrait of the self-deceived Emma succeeds so well because the driving force of irony is unimpeded.]

Emma is a throwing off of chains. The author and her characters move with a freedom and assurance unparalleled in Jane Austen's earlier work, and all the more astonishing by contrast with the uneasy stiffness of *Mansfield Park*. The new impetus is her old familiar one, but—from our first impression of *Emma*—purely assimilated to the medium as, in *Northanger Abbey* or even in *Pride and Prejudice*, it is not: the impetus is irony. In *Emma*, the sense of strain and anxiety is purged altogether. This time the author is in her novel and never out of it, never imposing upon us as in *Northanger Abbey* with her condescension or in *Pride and Prejudice* with her occasional prim moral reminders; and she is there for the comic artist's purpose only—to embody and direct our laughter.

The relaxation of an achieved technique is the very climate of *Emma*. Certainly, no other of Jane Austen's novels offers so pleasant and comfortable an atmosphere, so much the effect of an uncomplex and immediate art: wit, irony, light laughter shining in a triumph of surface. Its surface is, in fact, unmarred by a trace of self-justification, ill humor, or backsliding into morality. The story tells itself, and nothing seems more superfluous than inquiry or deep thought about it.

Emma, like *Pride and Prejudice*, is a story of self-deception, and the problem of each heroine is to undeceive herself. Yet Emma needs, not facts, but people, to help her. If Elizabeth Bennet is self-deceived under a set of special, doubtful circumstances, if she waits mainly for facts, Emma Woodhouse is a girl absolutely self-deceived, who takes and refashions whatever circumstances may arise, who can be checked only by a personality as positive as her own. We follow Emma's comic train of misunderstandings in the happy conviction that she cannot act otherwise until someone with will and intelligence takes her in hand—someone like Mr. Knightley, for example. We sympathize with Emma because she *must* fall in love, and we are relaxed because we know that she will. The love story in *Emma* is, then, predetermined to a degree unimaginable in *Pride and Prejudice*; for all Elizabeth needs in order to see is to have the facts before her, while Emma—in spite of her will and intelligence—cannot even begin to see clearly or steadily until Mr. Knightley tells her what is there.

Everything, it seems, is made as easy for us as for Mr. Woodhouse. Emma is provided from the beginning with a man not only admirable, but indispensable to her education. We need not worry about that. We have no financial anxiety: Emma is an "heiress of thirty thousand pounds." Rank is no problem: Emma is herself of an "ancient family," and her potential lover has an ancestry equally antique. Precedence is no problem: for Emma reigns alone at Hartfield and over Highbury, unencumbered by sisters, aunts, tyrannical parents or guardians, or petty nobility. Emma is, of course, habitually self-deceived; yet Mr. Knightley will come to the rescue: and we can read the novel, with no discomfort and only a pleasant minimum of suspense, as the ironic portrait of a girl who falls into mild self-deception and whose trustworthy friend always and finally helps her out.

—Marvin Mudrick, *Jane Austen: Irony as Defense and Discovery* (Princeton, N.J.: Princeton University Press, 1952): pp. 181–182.

WAYNE BOOTH ON THE IMPLIED AUTHOR

[Wayne Booth, an important critic from the University of Chicago, is the author of *The Rhetoric of Fiction,* the most influential theory of fiction of the 1960s. His other books include *Modern Dogma and the Rhetoric of Assent* and *A Rhetoric of Irony.* In this extract, Booth explains how the "omniscient" narrator in *Emma* wins our sympathy as a "friend and guide" we might be tempted to call "Jane Austen."]

We have seen how the inside views of the characters and the author's commentary have been used from the beginning to get the values straight and to keep them straight and to help direct our reactions to Emma. But we also see here a beautiful case of the dramatized author as friend and guide. "Jane Austen," like "Henry Fielding," is a paragon of wit, wisdom, and virtue. She does not talk about her qualities; unlike Fielding she does not in *Emma* call direct attention to her artistic skill. But we are seldom allowed to forget about her for all that. When we read this novel we accept her as representing everything we admire most. She is as generous and wise as Knightley; in fact, she is a shade more penetrating in her judgment. She is as subtle and witty as Emma would like to think herself. Without being sentimental she is in favor of tenderness. She is able to put an adequate but not excessive value on wealth and rank. She recognizes a fool when she sees one, but unlike Emma she knows that it is both immoral and foolish to be rude to fools. She is, in short, a perfect human being, within the concept of perfection established by the books she writes; she even recognizes that human perfection of the kind *she* exemplifies is not quite attainable in real life. The process of her domination is of course circular; her character establishes the values for us according to which her character is then found to be perfect. But this circularity does not affect the success of her endeavor; in fact it insures it.

Her "omniscience" is thus a much more remarkable thing than is ordinarily implied by the term. All good novelists know all about their characters—all that they need to know. And the question of how their narrators are to find out all that *they* need to know, the question of "authority," is a relatively simple one. The real choice is much more profound than this would imply. It is a choice of the moral, not merely the technical, angle of vision from which the story is to be told.

Unlike the central intelligences of James and his successors, "Jane Austen" has learned nothing at the end of the novel that she did not know at the beginning. She needed to learn nothing. She knew everything of importance already. We have been privileged to watch with her as she observes her favorite character climb from a considerably lower platform to join the exalted company of Knightley, "Jane Austen," and those of us readers who are wise enough, good enough, and perceptive enough to belong up there too. As Katherine Mansfield says, "the truth is that every true admirer of the novels cherishes the happy thought that he alone—reading between the lines—has become the secret friend of their author." Those who love "gentle Jane" as a secret friend may undervalue the irony and wit; those who see her in effect as the greatest of Shaw's heroines, flashing about her with the weapons of irony, may undervalue the emphasis on tenderness and good will. But only a very few can resist her.

The dramatic illusion of her presence as a character is thus fully as important as any other element in the story. When she intrudes, the illusion is not shattered. The only illusion we care about, the illusion of traveling intimately with a hardy little band of readers whose heads are screwed on tight and whose hearts are in the right place, is actually strengthened when we are refused the romantic love scene. Like the author herself, we don't care about the love scene. We can find love scenes in almost any novelist's works, but only here can we find a mind and heart that can give us clarity without oversimplification, sympathy and romance without sentimentality, and biting irony without cynicism.

—Wayne Booth, *The Rhetoric of Fiction* (Chicago: The University of Chicago Press, 1961): pp. 264–266.

ALISTAIR DUCKWORTH ON EMMA'S FREEDOM

[Alistair Duckworth is professor of English at the University of Florida, Gainsville. He is the author of studies of E. M. Forester and Jane Austen. In this excerpt, Duckworth describes how Emma's "unusual domestic power" and individualism lead to the "increasingly serious 'errors of the imagination'" that "endanger her own happiness and that of her circle of friends." Moreover, "beyond the personal, her imaginative errors have social and even epistemological implications."]

As many critics have noted, the setting of *Emma* is carefully chosen. Like Henry James, Jane Austen is interested in the problem of human freedom. What consequences will ensue, she asks, if, instead of describing a heroine in a position of insecurity as to her social place, I postulate an heiress as my central figure and give her complete freedom of action? Like Isabel Archer in *The Portrait of a Lady* after Ralph Touchett's legacy of £70,000, Emma is condemned to be free, as if by fictional fiat. "Handsome, clever, and rich"—her inheritance of £30,000 makes her a *bona fide* heiress in Jane Austen's financial scale—she differs from all previous Austen heroines in having no sense of insecurity, social or otherwise. At the center of a world apparently unendangered by any possibility of discontinuity, Emma's boundaries are where she wishes to place them.

The origins of Emma's subjectivism are therefore not so much Quixotic as familial. Her father is a senescent valetudinarian whose debility carries to an extreme the parental ineffectiveness that may be traced through the complacency of the Morland parents, the cynicism of Mr. Bennet, and the educational misconceptions of Sir Thomas Bertram. By his abrogation of all parental function— indeed by his lack of any evidence of masculinity—he has relinquished effective power over Hartfield to Emma. His stipulation against taking his position "at the bottom of the table" at the Hartfield dinner party for the Eltons is an index of his withdrawal from social and domestic responsibility. His only assertions are negatives: he wishes people would not marry, would not go out in the rain, would not overindulge in their eating; and his remedies are that everyone should stay single, remain beside their home firesides, and follow his own weak diet of thin gruel. Certainly, as Trilling has warned, it would be wrong to read Mr. Woodhouse's character too harshly. At least as important as his old-maidishness is his function as the recipient of Emma's piety. That she consistently honors her father is a major reason for our never losing faith in her fundamental goodness. Nevertheless her father's weakness is what permits Emma to assume unusual domestic power, so that when the "shadow" of Miss Taylor's authority leaves Hartfield, Emma's situation is one in which the "power of having rather too much her own way, and a disposition to think a little too well of herself" constitutes, as the narrator explicitly says, "real evils."

The evils of Emma's imagination resemble, but go beyond, those of Catherine Morland at Northanger. Like the "Gothic" heroine, Emma's intuitions are never wholly wrong. Indeed her snobbish dismissal of Mrs. Elton before she even sees her turns out to be a remarkably accurate prediction of her character, and Jane Fairfax does after all have a secret motive for coming to Highbury. As in Catherine's case, however, there is a difference between the sympathetic intuition of a truth and its exact intellectual formulation. Undisciplined by the rational faculty, the imagination may quickly distort the real nature of a situation. Emma's "genius for foretelling and guessing" may occasionally be a "poet's demand" that life be made more colorful than it is, but this faculty leads her into increasingly more serious misconceptions, as in each of the three movements of the novel she attempts not only to judge but to define her world from a center of self.

—Alistair Duckworth, *The Improvement of the Estate: A Study of Jane Austen's Novels* (Baltimore: The Johns Hopkins Press, 1971): pp. 148–149.

SUSAN MORGAN ON LOVE AND SELF-LOVE

[Susan Morgan is the author of *In the Meantime: Character and Perception in Jane Austen's Fiction,* from which this excerpt is taken. Morgan contrasts Emma's self-absorption and lack of self-knowledge with Mr. Knightley's regard for others.]

Emma always loves herself because she lives in her mind and it seems the world to her. She doesn't realize that others may also live in theirs. Her strange ignorance about her love for Mr. Knightley surely comes from that childish lack of discrimination in which all feelings are part of loving oneself. Not until she has to realize that Mr. Knightley can live in ways separate to his relation to her, ways that she would be excluded from, does she see his independence. Learning that Harriet has her own ideas for him, Emma is shocked into self-knowledge. "It darted through her, with the speed of an arrow, that Mr. Knightley must marry no one but herself!" When Emma was a little girl Mr. Knightley, like all adults, had been part of her domain (though he was distinctive in his critical view of her). But Emma grows up. She prompts Mr. Knightley's declaration and her own happiness by that new-learned consciousness which allows her to put his feelings ahead of her own. "Emma could not bear to give him pain. He was wishing to confide in her—

perhaps to consult her; —cost her what it would, she would listen." This is a classic scene in Austen's fiction. We see Emma's moral imagination at its best, in her selfless and generous sympathy for Mr. Knightley's point of view at the very moment she is filled with misery for her own. It is Emma's most imaginative act. Through it, we know she loves him and deserves him.

Mr. Knightley, it is true, also succumbs to the fault of judging another through the distorting perspective of his own interests. He is jealous. And hearing of Frank's engagement to Jane, he goes to comfort Emma, the "sweetest and best of all creatures, faultless in spite of all her faults." He had found her agitated and low.—Frank Churchill was a villain.—He heard her declare that she had never loved him. Frank Churchill's character was not desperate.—She was his own Emma, by hand and word, when they returned into the house; and if he could have thought of Frank Churchill then, he might have deemed him a very good sort of fellow." But apart from this endearing exception, Mr. Knightley is the one person who does consistently grant other people a personal existence.

Mr. Knightley is probably not more intelligent than Emma. Yet he often sees the true attitudes and situations of other people because he has acknowledged their internal lives apart from his wishes or plans. He is not just older than Emma, he has grown up. He recognizes social and material ambition in Mr. Elton and can think to send the carriage for Jane Fairfax because he sympathizes with her plight. His kindness to Miss Bates consists precisely in insisting on her right to recognition; on the dignity of being a separate person whose feelings must be taken into account. Miss Bates does not exist in order that Emma can make up a card table for her father. Mr. Knightley forces Emma to look at Miss Bates as a person rather than as a means, inconsequential in herself, of Emma's entertainment; to see her situation, to acknowledge that she had feelings which Emma has seriously hurt. It is a sad truth for the girl never loath to be first, but regardless of Emma, people will go about thinking their own thoughts, having their own emotions, and living their own lives. Even Miss Bates, however sunk in fortune, has a kingdom of her own.

—Susan Morgan, *In the Meantime: Character and Perception in Jane Austen's Fiction* (Chicago: University of Chicago Press, 1980): pp. 29–31.

Plot Summary of
Persuasion

Written in the last year of her life and published posthumously in 1818, *Persuasion* is Austen's most tender novel. A story of early regrets and second chances at love, its patient heroine, Anne Elliot, is said to resemble Austen herself. Frequently described as having a mellow, "autumnal" mood, the novel contains descriptions that are more poetically beautiful than those of Austen's other novels, suggesting the influence of the Romantic movement. Austen writes a happy ending for the only one of her heroines who has an unhappy past: Anne "had been forced into prudence in her youth, [but] she had learned romance as she grew older—the natural sequel of an unnatural beginning."

At age 27, Anne is considered destined for spinsterhood, since "her bloom had vanished early." Her father, Sir Walter Elliot, is obsessed with his pedigree and appearance, and pays little attention to her. Her mother died when she was 14, and since then her beautiful older sister Elizabeth has presided haughtily over the household. Twenty-nine and herself unmarried, Elizabeth, her father's favorite, shares his vanity and snobbishness. Their peevish younger sister Mary is married to Charles Musgrove, the good-natured oldest son of a property-owning family in the neighborhood.

Unable to curb his spending, Sir Walter finds himself in financial straits. Lady Russell, a close friend and Anne's beloved godmother, advises him to lease Kellynch Hall, the family estate, and go to Bath. Sir Walter leaves with Elizabeth and her friend Mrs. Clay, whom Anne suspects of scheming to marry her father, and Kellynch is occupied by Admiral and Mrs. Croft. Mrs. Croft's brother, we learn, is Captain Frederick Wentworth, a name Anne is startled to hear.

Anne had met Frederick Wentworth eight years before, when he was a young naval officer, "full of life and ardour" but penniless, and they had fallen in love. Lady Russell believed the connection was imprudent and persuaded Anne to break the engagement. She felt it was important that Anne marry someone of higher rank and greater wealth. Anne, young and impressionable, could not resist this strong "persuasion" from a trusted adviser, but suffered deeply from the loss: "her attachment and regret had, for a long time, clouded every enjoyment of youth; and an early loss of bloom and spirits had been their lasting effect."

Anne, unneeded and unmissed by her father and older sister, goes to spend time with Mary. Mary's unpretentious, hospitable in-laws live next door with their high-spirited daughters Henrietta and Louisa Musgrove. To Anne's dismay, and the Musgrove sisters' delight, they hear that Captain Wentworth has come to visit the Crofts. In the years since she knew him, Wentworth has become a wealthy man, and he is very desirable in the eyes of the young women. Anne faces their inevitable meeting with great trepidation, avoiding him as long as she can.

The dreaded moment arrives and Wentworth is cold:

> He had not forgiven Anne Elliot. She had used him ill; deserted and disappointed him; and worse, she had shown a feebleness of character in doing so, which his own decided, confident temper could not endure. She had given him up to oblige others. It had been the effect of overpersuasion. It had been weakness and timidity.

Wentworth resents Anne and intends to marry someone else. Both of the Musgrove sisters appear to be smitten with him, and he is soon suspected of courting Louisa. Socializing in this small circle brings Anne and Wentworth together frequently, and she is mortified, but gradually they develop a warmer rapport. In one moment when her two-year-old nephew is clinging to her, Wentworth picks up the child and Anne is painfully aware of his tenderness and physical closeness. On a long autumn walk, she observes him talking animatedly with Louisa, however, and resigns herself once again to a bitter loss. Louisa is impetuous and eager, in stark contrast to Anne's over-cautious behavior years before.

The group decides to take a trip to Lyme Regis, an ocean resort where Wentworth has friends. Anne meets the odd and melancholy Captain Benwick, who is mourning his fiancée's tragic death, and counsels him not to read too much poetry. Louisa soon displays that her impetuousness is not always preferable to prudence: playfully jumping from a seawall while flirting with Wentworth, she falls and knocks herself unconscious. In the panic that ensues, Anne takes charge and Wentworth admires her composure. Louisa is conveyed to the home of Wentworth's friend, Captain Harville (whose sister was Benwick's fiancée), and they are assured that Louisa will make a slow but steady recovery. Wentworth is anguished, feeling responsible for her injury, and Anne interprets his emotion as love for Louisa.

As **Volume II** opens, Anne is alone with her "silent, pensive self," depressed to think of Louisa's future with Wentworth. She is slightly cheered, but more embarrassed, to learn that Captain Benwick has shown signs of being infatuated with her. Anne travels to Bath, where she is even more lonely in the company of her father and sister, who ignore her. With her genuine feeling and appreciation of intelligent conversation, she dislikes the "elegant stupidity of private parties." The fuss her father and sister make over rank and wealth, exemplified in their obsequious treatment of Dowager Viscountess Dalrymple, underscores the triviality of their concerns. The other side of Bath is revealed when Anne meets an old school friend, Mrs. Smith, now a poor widow and invalid.

Sir Walter and Elizabeth are especially gratified by an acquaintance with William Elliot, Sir Walter's heir, who is surprisingly attentive after years of neglect. He turns out to have observed Anne in Lyme Regis and found her attractive (her color heightened by the sea air) and suavely tries to win her affections. Lady Russell is eager for the match to succeed, wishing to see Anne as Lady Elliot, the mistress of Kellynch. Anne herself is suspicious of Mr. Elliot's motives. He is "too generally agreeable," and although he is "rational, discreet, polished," he is not open.

Mary sends an excited letter: Louisa is engaged to marry Captain Benwick. For Anne, the news is "almost too wonderful for belief" since it means that Wentworth is free. He arrives in Bath soon thereafter, and Anne suspects that his feelings for her may have revived. She finds herself in a state of terrible suspense, feeling "agitation, pain, pleasure, a something between delight and misery." At an evening concert, she at last has an opportunity to speak with him, and he expresses "his opinion of Louisa Musgrove's inferiority . . . his feelings as to a first, strong attachment—sentences begun which he could not finish—his half-averted eyes, and more than half-expressive glance—all, all declared that he had a heart returning to her. . . . " Anne is overjoyed, and begins to "bloom" again: "Her happiness was from within. Her eyes were bright, and her cheeks glowed."

Rumors have circulated, however, that Anne is engaged to William Elliot, and when he maneuvers to sit beside her, Wentworth looks grave. She wonders desperately how she can assure Wentworth that his fears are unfounded. Anne soon learns from Mrs. Smith that William Elliot is an unscrupulous fortune-hunter who has apparently come to Bath to prevent Mrs. Clay from marrying Sir Walter and ensure his inheritance. William Elliot and Mrs. Clay are observed in a secret rendezvous, and their motives remain nebulous.

When the Musgroves arrive in Bath, their cheerful turmoil at last affords Anne the opportunity to express her feelings. She finds Wentworth and Captain Harville at the Musgrove's lodgings. In this climactic scene, Wentworth is busy writing a letter, and Anne has a moving conversation with Captain Harville about constancy in love, within Wentworth's earshot. Harville is astonished with the rest of them that Benwick has gotten over his sister so quickly. Anne maintains that *women* who have truly loved remain faithful, though men's feelings change more easily. In a poignant reflection on her own circumstances, she explains that women "live at home, quiet, confined, and our feelings prey upon us," whereas men move in the world and can readily forget love. Harville argues to the contrary, claiming that men's feelings are stronger, "capable of beating most rough usage, and riding out the heaviest weather." After all, literature affords many examples of fickle women. Cautioning against examples in books, Anne rejoins, "Men have had every advantage of us in telling their own story . . . ; the pen has been in their hands." Their discussion has far-reaching implications for interpreting Austen's views of gender and authorship.

Anne is unaware that as she speaks, Wentworth is writing a letter to her. Its contents bring "overpowering happiness" as he declares his love openly and passionately: "I offer myself to you again with a heart even more your own than when you almost broke it eight years and a half ago." She responds quickly, and they express their mutual happiness and hopes for the future. As

Austen's narrator puts it, "Who can be in doubt of what followed?" The expected marriage will take place, but Wentworth and Anne's mature love also suggests new possibilities. She will lead a varied and exciting life as the wife of a naval officer, escaping the stifling world of her father's home. In this novel, where the old order is made laughable and the hero represents a world of risk and movement, Austen concludes not by confirming traditional values as she does in her other novels, but by gesturing toward new territory. ❀

List of Characters in
Persuasion

In her youth, **Anne Elliot** was "an extremely pretty girl, with gentleness, modesty, taste, and feeling," but she is faded at 27, even "haggard," in her father's view. Deeply regretting that she broke off an early love affair with Captain Wentworth because she was persuaded it was unsuitable, she resigns herself to loneliness, fully versed in "the art of knowing our own nothingness beyond our own circle." Even within her circle, she is under-appreciated. Unassertive, reserved, self-sacrificing, she has an "elegance of mind and sweetness of character" that often go unnoticed. Her mildness, compassion, and good sense are apparent to Captain Wentworth, however, and their reawakened love leads to her second "bloom." Like Wentworth, Anne prizes "the frank, the open-hearted, the eager character beyond all others. Warmth and enthusiasm did captivate her still."

Captain Frederick Wentworth has "a great deal of intelligence, spirit and brilliancy." A penniless naval officer when he first met and fell in love with Anne, eight years before the novel's action begins, he has since made his fortune on foreign voyages. Adventurous and energetic, he possesses an innate confidence that is "powerful in its own warmth, and bewitching in the wit which often expressed it." Capable of being resentful and headstrong, he nonetheless demonstrates a "sanguine temper [and] fearlessness of mind." His emotional resilience and profound loyalty enable him to renew his relationship with Anne.

Sir Walter Elliot is a "foolish, spendthrift baronet, who had not had principle or sense enough to maintain himself in the situation in which Providence had placed him." Austen is explicit: "Vanity was the beginning and the end of Sir Walter Elliot's character; vanity of person and of situation. He had been remarkably handsome in his youth; and, at 54, was still a very fine man. Few women could think more of their personal appearance than he did." Fond of looking at himself in the mirror and looking up his name in the Baronetage, he provides a comical portrait of self-importance and outdated, trivialized values.

Mary Musgrove, Anne's younger sister, is a hypochondriac and whiner ("my sore-throats, you know, are always worse than anybody's"). Unlike her self-controlled sister Anne, Mary "had not resources for solitude; and, inheriting a considerable share of the Elliot self-importance, was very prone to add to every other distress that of fancying herself neglected and ill-used." As she writes self-pityingly in a letter to Anne, "I am always out of the way when anything desirable is going on." She has two boisterous young boys and an exceptionally tolerant husband.

Lady Russell is "a sensible, deserving woman . . . of steady age and character." Overly concerned with rank and cautious about appearances, she advises Anne not to marry Wentworth. For the most part, she is well-meaning and genuinely fond of Anne, but insists on being "most correct in her conduct, strict in her notions of decorum, and with manners that were held a standard of good breeding. She had a cultivated mind, and was, generally speaking, rational and consistent—but she had prejudices on the side of ancestry; she had a value for rank and consequence, which blinded her a little to the faults of those who possessed them." ❀

Critical Views on
Persuasion

DAVID MONAGHAN ON THE BREAKDOWN OF MANNERS

[David Monaghan is professor of English at Mount St. Vincent University in Halifax, Nova Scotia. He is the author of *Jane Austen in a Social Context* and *The Novels of John Le Carré*. In this excerpt, Monaghan demonstrates that the social order that Sir Walter Elliot represents, now corrupted by hypocrisy, vanity, and even depravity, cannot be redeemed by the novel's conclusion.]

Since external display is so important to Jane Austen, both at an individual and a social level, its loss of function in *Persuasion* must be taken as an important indication that in this novel she is aware that the old order is rapidly losing its prestige and authority. In direct contrast to any of her other heroines, Anne Elliot has achieved maturity by the time the novel opens. However, she does not find herself in harmony with her community as they finally do because manners have ceased to serve as a medium for moral communication in the two social milieus with which she becomes involved: that of Kellynch has degenerated into a decadent condition because of its acceptance of external display as an end in itself, while that which embraces the Musgroves and the naval characters lacks a mature comprehension of the importance of formal behavior, although it retains a basic sense of duty and obligation to others. As a result both have lost the ability to judge readily the merits of their members and fail to afford Anne the position of consequence she deserves. In such a world Anne cannot, of course, look to the formal social occasion to facilitate her lonely pilgrimage in search of love and acceptance. Instead she had to rely on the chance occurrence of situations sufficiently testing to give her the opportunity of actively proving herself to the Musgroves, Harvilles, and, above all, to Wentworth. Consequently, there is an element of luck involved in Anne's final acceptance into the Musgrove world and reunion with Wentworth that is missing from any of Jane Austen's other novels. While Marianne Dashwood or an Emma Woodhouse enters almost automatically into a harmonious relationship with her world once she has corrected personal faults, Anne Elliot, perhaps the most mature of all the heroines, has to rely on a child's broken collarbone and a young woman's fall to provide her with opportunities to demonstrate her worth.

Although this breakdown in the structure of manners is indicative of the passing of the old order, Jane Austen does not introduce what would seem to be an appropriate elegiac note into the conclusion of *Persuasion*. Instead she tries to reconcile herself to the changes that are taking place by finally accepting her heroine's rejection of formality and subsequent rationalization that the new world into which she is entering is a fully satisfactory one. Because of her experiences with her father, whose life has been reduced to "a . . . vacuous ceremony" by his overriding conviction that rank and personal appearance constitute in themselves criteria for judging people, with William Walter Elliot, who utilizes a polite facade to mask his real depravity, and with the Musgroves, Harvilles, and Crofts, who lack her father's polished manners but retain a basic comprehension of their social duty, Anne comes to the conclusion that refinement and sincerity are almost inevitably irreconcilable. As a response to her own world, Austen's judgment is a reasonable one. However, if one bears in mind the crucial role that Jane Austen assigns to manners as the generators and preservers of good moral standards in her other novels, Anne is not justified in concluding that society based upon a structure of manners must necessarily be hypocritical and shallow. The social group into which Anne is finally admitted has many good qualities and is certainly to be preferred to her own family. But, lacking the ability to judge by more objective standards than familial affection or professional esteem, it remains rather chaotic and disorganized and must be considered inferior to such harmonious and beautifully ordered worlds as Highbury. Thus, in order to acquiesce finally with Anne's position, Jane Austen is forced to reject implicitly the value of the social structure which she extols so convincingly in her novels and to ignore much of what she has established throughout this novel.

—David Monaghan, "The Decline of the Gentry: A Study of Jane Austen's Attitude to Formality in *Persuasion*," *Studies in the Novel* 7, no. 1 (Spring 1975): pp. 76–77.

GENE RUOFF ON THE NOVEL'S ENDING

[Gene Ruoff, professor of English at the University of Illinois at Chicago, is the editor, with Karl Kroeber, of *Romantic Poetry: Recent Revisionary Criticism* and the author of *Wordsworth and Coleridge: The Making of the Major Lyrics.* Observing that *Persuasion,* unlike Austen's other novels, does not end with a strong sense of community, Ruoff suggests that Austen has grown less optimistic about the continuity of cultural memory.]

The ending of *Persuasion* is especially severe in its exclusions: it brushes aside all the Elliots except Anne, all the Musgroves, and even one naval officer, Captain Benwick, who had become engaged to Louisa Musgrove. We might, therefore, expect it to be equally exacting in its grounds for friendship, an issue which has commanded Jane Austen's attention since the juvenilia. Without a fixed geographical center, proximity can play no role in these newly formed relationships, nor to a large degree do a number of other familiar Austenian bonding agents—blood ties, cultural backgrounds, ages, and even dispositions. For all this, the figures who come together seem somehow solider than those who have closed the other novels. *Persuasion* embraces fewer charming eccentrics and tolerates fewer bores, and it proposes few startling reformations after the close of its dramatic action: no Kitty to be "improved," no Marianne to learn to love Colonel Brandon, no Sir Thomas Bertram to gain a rejuvenated sense of parental responsibility. At the end of both *Pride and Prejudice* and *Mansfield Park,* one is left with the feeling that the communities formed are stronger than either the individuals within them or the relationships among them would ordinarily allow. Problematical characters, weak and immature but not evil, are propped up by the related supporters of generational continuity and landed property. In making do without these supports, *Persuasion* asks considerably more of its characters. The sort of parental incompetence tolerated in Mrs. Dashwood, the Bennets, and the Bertrams, for example, is not acceptable in the case of the elder Musgroves, even though they are generally pleasant and well meaning. Harmlessness is not on the novel's list of approved virtues.

In seeking the grounds of community in *Persuasion,* one might recall that a primary function of the estate in the earlier endings was to stimulate familial and cultural memory. The emotions engendered by the portrait gallery at Pemberley display this role at its most successful, just as the disarray into which Mansfield is thrown in Sir Thomas's absence shows its failure. Sir Thomas's response to the desecration of his billiard room dwells in a complicated way on the issue of family memory: "he felt it too much indeed for many words; and having shaken hands with Edmund, meant to try to lose the disagreeable impression, and forget how much he had been forgotten himself as soon as he could, after the house had been cleared of every object enforcing the remembrance, and restored to its proper state." This is the sort of word game through which Jane Austen often depicts the self-deluded. Upset by a failure of family memory, Sir Thomas tries to forget it by wiping out its visible signs. Obliterating this "disagreeable impression," of course, leads ultimately to others even more disagreeable, which will be less easily forgotten. An excessive reliance on houses or objects in general for recollection can be tricky business, as prone to generate the self-indulgent and wallowing joys of nostalgia—one vice from which Fanny Price herself is not quite free—as vital and effective memories. *Persuasion* is even more centrally concerned with the vagaries of remembering and forgetting than *Mansfield Park,* but along with the estate it does without the various keepsakes and tokens which are Fanny's treasures in the old school room. *Persuasion* places its highest value on the power of the individual memory, which, in the absence of such mnemonic aids as a stable home and family, must itself provide the continuity essential to the formation of a new community.

—Gene Ruoff, "Anne Elliot's Dowry: Reflections on the Ending of *Persuasion,*" *The Wordsworth Circle* 7, no. 4 (Autumn 1976): pp. 345–346.

[Tony Tanner is an influential critic of English and American novelists, especially Conrad, Pynchon, and James. His studies include *Adultery in the Novel: Contract and Transgression* and *The Reign of Wonder: Naivety and Reality in American Literature*. In this excerpt, Tanner compares Anne's "in-between" status to Sir Walter Elliot's absorption in signs of his own identity.]

Persuasion. Not "Persuasion and . . ."—Resistance, Refusal, Rebellion, for instance. Just *Persuasion.* In previous titles using abstract nouns Jane Austen had deployed pairs. This time the debate, the struggle, the contestation, the contrarieties and ambiguities are all in the one word. As they are all in, or concentrated on, the one girl. Anne Elliot is the loneliest of Jane Austen's heroines. Persuaded by others, she has to repersuade herself. 〈. . .〉

Jane Austen opens her book with the description of a man looking at a book in which he reads the same words as her book opens with—"Elliot, of Kellynch-hall". This is the kind of teasing regression which we have become accustomed to in contemporary writers but which no one associates with the work of Jane Austen. It alerts us to at least two important considerations [of] the dangers involved in seeking validation and self-justification in 〈a〉 book as opposed to life, in record rather than in action, in name as opposed to function; and the absolutely negative "vanity" (her key word for Sir Walter) in looking for and finding one's familial and social position, one's reality, in an inscription rather than in a pattern of behaviour, in a sign rather than the range of responsibilities which it implicitly signifies. We learn how fond Sir Walter is of mirrors and how hopelessly and hurtfully unaware of the real needs and feelings of his dependents he is. This opening situation poses someone fixed in an ultimate solipsism gazing with inexhaustible pleasure into the textual mirror which simply gives him back his name. The opening of Jane Austen's text—a title, a name, a domicile, a geographic location—implies a whole series of unwritten obligations and responsibilities related to rank, family, society and the very land itself, none of which Sir Walter, book-bound and self-mesmerised, either keeps or recognises. He is only interested in himself and what reflects him—mirrors or daughters. Thus he likes Elizabeth because she is "very like himself"—this is parenthood as narcissism—and Mary has "acquired a little artificial importance" because she has married into a tolerably respectable family; "but Anne, with an elegance of mind and sweetness of character, which must have placed her high with any people of real understanding, was nobody with either father or sister: her word had no weight; her convenience was always to give way;—she was only Anne". Only Anne—no rank, no effective surname, no house, no location; her words are weightless, and physically speaking she always has to "give way"—that is, accept perpetual displacement. Anne we may call the girl on the threshold, existing in that limboid space between the house of the father which has to be left and the house of the husband which has yet to be found. No longer a child and not yet a wife, Anne is, precisely, in between, and she lives in in-betweenness. She is a speaker who is unheard; she is a body who is a "nobody". I emphasise this because the problems of the body who is, socially speaking, a nobody were to engage many of the great nineteenth-century writers.

—Tony Tanner, *Jane Austen* (London: Macmillan, 1986): pp. 208–209.

Marilyn Butler on Conservatism and the Gentry

[Marilyn Butler, professor of English literature at King's College, Cambridge, is an important New Historicist critic whose books include *Romantics, Rebels, and Reactionaries* and *Jane Austen and the War of Ideas.* In this excerpt, Butler stresses the importance of providing a political context for Austen's novels and broadly describes the period of political and literary reaction in which she wrote.]

An account of Austen's politics that relied too heavily on the conclusions of the political scientist, anthropologist, or social historian would be unduly reverential to generalities, over the specific evidence available in her individual case; but to glean her opinions from her writings without attention to her circumstances is equally unsatisfactory. She thought, and changed her thinking, along with certain groups in society, who were living, as it happens, through a time of national crisis: the gentry, and also gentry hangers-on in southern England; the Church of England, and that church's Evangelical movement. She was also a novelist, and a woman novelist, when sharp ideological pressures were being felt by writers. A full reading of the novels recognizes their rich life in time and place. ⟨. . .⟩

Austen began to write in the mid-1790s, at a point when the arts were moving into a period of conservatism. The most obvious reason for this was the French Revolution, a movement with enormous intellectual élan that quickly exported subversion and republicanism to neighboring countries. The Low Countries, Switzerland, the Rhineland, Italy, and Spain quickly fell to the French; Britain, Prussia, Austria, and Russia resisted, and armed themselves spiritually to resist, with ideas dubbed already at the time as a "counterrevolution." Quite apart from fear of the French and what they currently stood for, there were forces working for conservatism in both British and German society. Steadily increasing prosperity swelled the number of leisured classes, bringing with them more of the urban bourgeoisie and younger branches of gentry families like the Austens, who in other times might have sunk. These people were naturally suspicious of the values of the established upper classes—fashionable, frivolous, mannered, "French." Guarding the homelands against innovation and keeping the propertied in the saddle entailed dispensing with much of the culture of the previous era, including sensibility and primitivism in its more political forms. The very concept of art as a carrier of "Opinion," so universal in the Enlightenment, passed quickly out of fashion. Even Shelley, most insistently radical of poets, was soon declaring, "Didactic poetry is my abhorrence." It became more reputable and serious to portray man alone, or communing with God or Nature, not man in society.

The novel in Austen's lifetime took a different aesthetic route from poetry, though equally in the direction of political conservatism or quietism. As novels were written by women and other amateurs, to claim that the form existed to express the writer's inner life or personal aspirations would have been undesirable. On the contrary, it was often stressed that most novels had been too indulgent to women's dreams and aspirations. The fashion of focusing on a protagonist's inner life gave place to a concern with the conditions of external life; fantasy and the gothic, to a more closely documented treatment of history and society, notably Scott's. The best critics of the novel of Austen's heyday—Jeffrey, Croker, Ward, Foster, Scott himself—agreed that the significant modern technical innovation in the novel was a minute realism, fidelity to the facts as they were.

—Marilyn Butler, "History, Politics, and Religion." In *The Jane Austen Companion* (New York: Macmillan Publishing Company, 1986): pp. 191–193.

JOHN WILTSHIRE ON BATH AND THE SOCIAL BODY

[John Wiltshire is professor of English at La Trobe University and the author of *Samuel Johnson in the Medical World: The Doctor and the Patient,* and *Jane Austen and the Body,* from which this extract is taken. Wiltshire argues that Bath society showcases healthy and attractive bodies but also discloses the less pleasant medical and economic realities that characters like Sir Walter Elliot attempt to ignore.]

Bath's *raison d'etre* and subsequent prosperity was based upon its hot springs and medicinal waters. By Jane Austen's time it had become a resort which combined facilities for the renovation of health, and venues for the pursuit of social and sexual liaisons, a place in which the medicinal and the erotic were intertwined—an eighteenth-century Magic Fountain. "Where the waters do agree, it is quite wonderful the relief they give", Mrs Elton tells Emma, and compounds the impertinence by adding "And as to its recommendations to *you,* I fancy I need not take much pains to dwell on them. The advantages of Bath to the young are pretty generally understood". Mrs Smith is one of those among its visitors who is lodging there for the purpose of health; she has come on the—arguably rational—grounds that the hot baths will relieve, if not cure, her rheumatism. But Bath had been for many years, as Defoe declared, "the resort of the sound rather than the sick", and its culture as an elegant watering place treats the body in another mode. The body is perceived as an object; it's to be prized and appraised, like handsome furniture, as a commodity. Thus when Elizabeth Elliot bestows a card upon Wentworth, her gesture is not a sign of forgiveness or reconciliation, a prompting of the inner moral life: "The truth was, that Elizabeth had been long enough in Bath, to understand the importance of a man of such an air and appearance as his. The past was nothing. The present was that Captain Wentworth would move about well in her drawing room". The male body becomes an item of social circulation here as much as the female has always been, as for example at Netherfield. It is thus easy to elide Sir Walter Elliot's narcissism and vanity into representative status, as he stands "in a shop in Bond-street" counting handsome faces as they go by. In its drawing rooms and evening parties the values he articulates can be seen to be reified, and he commodifies people on the streets as Lady Russell appraises handsome curtains. ⟨. . .⟩

Bath and the Elliots are linked in a metonymic relationship, and the rest of the novel has a contrastive and interrogative function towards the corpus of values they represent. Bath excludes nature, excludes the labouring and serving classes, and attempts to repress the knowledge of growth and change, of decay and death. Sir Walter lives out an infantile fantasy of narcissistic omnipotence. Bath society represses that knowledge of the body as an unstable and imperfect subjective condition upon which its economy initially wholly, and still in part, depends, just as the labouring classes and wilderness are expunged from its spaces. But the novel discloses a "real world" both inside and outside Bath in which the reader's attention is constantly being drawn to these necessary conditions of human life, to what Lady Russell calls "the uncertainty of all human events and calculation" and especially to thoughts about the human body very different from his simple equation of handsomeness and value.

—John Wiltshire, *Jane Austen and the Body* (Cambridge: Cambridge University Press, 1992): pp. 160–162.

Works by Jane Austen

Sense and Sensibility. 1811.

Pride and Prejudice. 1813.

Mansfield Park. 1814.

Emma. 1816.

Persuasion. 1818.

Northanger Abbey. 1818.

Works about
Jane Austen

Auerbach, Nina. "O Brave New World: Evolution and Revolution in *Persuasion*." *ELH* 39 (1972): 112–128.

Austen, Jane. *Jane Austen's Letters to Her Sister Cassandra and Others,* ed. R. W. Chapman. New York: Oxford University Press, 1952.

Austen-Leigh, J. E. *A Memoir of Jane Austen.* London: Bentley, 1870, and R. W. Chapman, ed., Oxford: Clarendon Press, 1926.

Batey, Mavis. *Jane Austen and the English Landscape.* London: Barn Elms, 1996.

Bloom, Harold, ed. *Jane Austen.* New York: Chelsea House, 1986.

———, ed. *Jane Austen's Emma.* New York: Chelsea House, 1987.

———, ed. *Jane Austen's Mansfield Park.* New York: Chelsea House, 1986.

———, ed. *Jane Austen's Pride and Prejudice.* New York: Chelsea House, 1987.

Booth, Wayne. *The Rhetoric of Fiction.* Chicago: University of Chicago Press, 1961.

Bradbrook, Frank. *Jane Austen and her Predecessors.* Cambridge: Cambridge University Press, 1967.

Brown, Julia Prewitt. *Jane Austen's Novels: Social Change and Literary Form.* Cambridge: Harvard University Press, 1979.

Butler, Marilyn. "History, Politics, and Religion." In *The Jane Austen Companion.* New York: Macmillan, 1986.

———. *Jane Austen and the War of Ideas.* Oxford: Oxford University Press, 1975.

Chandler, Alice. "'A Pair of Fine Eyes': Jane Austen's Treatment of Sex." *Studies in the Novel* 7, no. 1 (Spring 1975): 88–103.

Chapman, R. W. *Jane Austen: Facts and Problems.* Oxford: Clarendon Press, 1948.

Devlin, David. *Jane Austen and Education.* New York: Barnes & Noble Books, 1975.

Duckworth, Alistair. *The Improvement of the Estate: A Study of Jane Austen's Novels.* Baltimore: Johns Hopkins Press, 1971.

Fergus, Jan. *Jane Austen and the Didactic Novels: Northanger Abbey, Sense and Sensibility, and Pride and Prejudice.* Totowa, N.J.: Barnes & Noble Books, 1983.

Gilbert, Sandra M., and Susan Gubar. *The Madwoman in the Attic: The Woman Writer and the Nineteenth-Century Literary Imagination.* New Haven: Yale University Press, 1979.

Grey, J. David, A. Walton Litz, and B. C. Southam, eds. *The Jane Austen Companion.* New York: Macmillan, 1986.

Halperin, John. *The Life of Jane Austen.* Sussex: Harvester Press, 1984.

Johnson, Claudia. *Jane Austen: Women, Politics, and the Novel.* Chicago: University of Chicago Press, 1988.

Kirkham, Margaret. *Jane Austen: Feminism and Fiction.* Totowa, N.J.: Barnes & Noble Books, 1983.

Kroeber, Karl. *Studies in Fictional Structure: The Art of Jane Austen, Charlotte Brontë, George Eliot.* Princeton: Princeton University Press, 1971.

Litz, A. Walton. *Jane Austen: A Study of her Artistic Development.* New York: Oxford University Press, 1965.

McMaster, Juliet. *Jane Austen on Love.* Victoria, British Columbia: University of Victoria Press, 1978.

Monaghan, David. "The Decline of the Gentry: A Study of Jane Austen's Attitude to Formality in *Persuasion*," *Studies in the Novel* 7, no. 1 (Spring 1975): 73–87.

———. *Jane Austen: Structure and Social Vision.* London: Macmillan & Co., 1980.

Morgan, Susan. *In the Meantime: Character and Perception in Jane Austen's Fiction.* Chicago: University of Chicago Press, 1980.

Mudrick, Marvin. *Jane Austen: Irony as Defense and Discovery.* Princeton, N.J.: Princeton University Press, 1952.

Nardin, Jane. *Those Elegant Decorums: The Concept of Propriety in Jane Austen's Novels.* Albany, N.Y.: State University of New York Press, 1973.

Page, Norman. *The Language of Jane Austen*. New York: Barnes & Noble, 1972.

Piggott, Patrick. *The Innocent Diversion: A Study of Music in the Life and Writings of Jane Austen*. London: Douglas Cleverdon, 1979.

Poovey, Mary. *The Proper Lady and the Woman Writer: Ideology as Style in the Works of Mary Wollstonecraft, Mary Shelley, and Jane Austen*. Chicago: University of Chicago Press, 1984.

Roberts, Warren. *Jane Austen and the French Revolution*. New York: St. Martin's Press, 1979.

Ruoff, Gene. "Anne Elliot's Dowry: Reflections on the Ending of *Persuasion*." *The Wordsworth Circle* 7, no. 4 (Autumn 1976): 342–351.

Said, Edward. "Jane Austen and Empire." In *Culture and Imperialism*. New York: Alfred A. Knopf, 1993.

Southam, B. C. *Jane Austen*. Essex: Longman Group Ltd., 1975.

———. ed. *Jane Austen: The Critical Heritage*. New York: Routledge, 1995.

Tanner, Tony. *Jane Austen*. London: Macmillan, 1986.

Troost, Linda, and Sayre Greenfield, eds. *Jane Austen in Hollywood*. Lexington: The University Press of Kentucky, 1998.

Watt, Ian, ed. *Critical Jane Austen: A Collection of Essays*. Englewood Cliffs, N.J.: Prentice-Hall, 1963.

———. *The Rise of the Novel*. Berkeley: University of California Press, 1957.

Wiltshire, John. *Jane Austen and the Body*. Cambridge: Cambridge University Press, 1992.

Wood, Nigel, ed. *Mansfield Park*. Philadelphia: Open University Press, 1993.

Index of
Themes and Ideas